THE SCENT OF THE COUNTRYSIDE

THE SCENT OF THE COUNTRYSIDE

DORIS E. GAWRYS

ISIS
LARGE PRINT
Oxford

First published in Great Britain 2010
by
ISIS Publishing Ltd.

Published in Large Print 2010 by ISIS Publishing Ltd.,
7 Centremead, Osney Mead, Oxford OX2 0ES
by arrangement with
The Author

British Library Cataloguing in Publication Data
Gawrys, Doris.
    The scent of the countryside. - - (Reminiscence)
    1. Gawrys, Doris - - Childhood and youth.
    2. Rayleigh (England) - - Social life and customs.
    3. Rayleigh (England) - - Biography.
    4. Large type books.
    I. Title II. Series
    942.6'775082'092–dc22

ISBN 978–0–7531–9592–5 (hb)
ISBN 978–0–7531–9593–2 (pb)

Printed and bound in Great Britain by
T. J. International Ltd., Padstow, Cornwall

This book is dedicated to my dear parents,
Robert and Eva Rogers, who made my life
so happy and to the memory of my dear
cousin, Mollie.

Nostalgia

Memory takes me to the meadows
Where I'm a child again
Roaming in the sunshine
Running thro' the rain
Along the tangled hedgerows
With straggling winding briar
The leaves fresh green in Springtime
In Autumn red as fire.

I learned to know the Blackbird
The Yellowhammer too
The soaring singing Skylark
And the grass all wet with dew.
The scent of wild roses
And honeysuckle sweet
Bees buzzing in the clover
And daises at my feet.

Ripened corn-stalks whispered
In gentle summer breeze
Scarlet poppies bobbing
All around my knees.
Falling leaves in Autumn
Yellow, red and gold
Covering the seedlings
When Winter's grip takes hold.

Fields all white with snowfall
Snowflakes in the air
Ice ferns on the window-panes
And trees all stark and bare.
Nature's wondrous bounty
In my memory's store
Treasures of my childhood
Mine for evermore.

Written by the author in memory of Pengelly,
her childhood home.

Introduction

Pengelly was the name of the house where I spent my early childhood. Of all the many people who knew and loved Pengelly, only my cousin Phyllis remains to share her memories with me. One only has to say Pengelly and we are transported back to the time when each day was an adventure, when the joy of being alive was a tangible thing to be held and savoured.

Whenever conversation turns to "the good old days", those of my own generation become wistful, whilst the younger ones find a special enchantment about the way we lived then. My little anecdotes have interested and given pleasure to so many people, that it occurred to me that I should write them down, for when I depart this life, they will be lost forever. They are told simply, through the eyes of a child, the way I saw them.

When one considers that in the early 1920s a crystal wireless set was the very latest thing to have in the home, and that since then we have progressed to the television and video and computer, aeroplanes that fly across the world in a day, men landing on the moon and Space Shuttles, oil rigs in the sea, vaccines which have virtually wiped out epidemic diseases and so many more wonderful, and sometimes terrifying inventions, it is not surprising that life in the year 2000 would, to me as a child, have been pure fantasy. So in its way, my simple life has it's own magic for those who cannot imagine life without these advancements.

I dedicate these memories to my dear parents who made my life at Pengelly so happy and taught me to appreciate the things money cannot buy.

CHAPTER
ONE

My father snipped a rose from the bush and handed it to me saying, "Isn't that beautiful?"

"M-m-m, lovely," I said. "The perfume takes me back to Pengelly."

"Really? Why?" he asked, smiling.

"The white rose by the front door. I used to walk round it sniffing the air; I could almost taste its fragrance. Do you remember the Periwinkle that grew over the fallen tree trunk in the front garden?"

"Yes I do; very pretty wasn't it?" he replied.

"I remember the day we moved to Pengelly," I said. "At least, I think I do. It is more an impression than a memory. I was wearing a blue bonnet and coat trimmed with white fur, and for some reason I was lying on the floor in the corner of the kitchen. By my side was a baby and we were wrapped in someone's coat. To my right was a wall papered in yellow with sprigs of pink flowers and at my head a cupboard extended from floor to ceiling. It was growing dark, and I could see the legs of people passing to and fro."

"That's remarkable. You were just two years old, and you are absolutely right," Father said. "The removal men had lost their way, and we made a makeshift bed on the floor for you and Mollie. They eventually arrived at dusk, and it must have been them you saw bringing in the furniture."

"You are right about the coat and bonnet too," my mother added. "I made them for you, only they were trimmed with swansdown not fur."

This conversation took place about forty years after we had left Pengelly. To have my earliest memories confirmed pleased me very much. I hold in my mind's eye coloured pictures, which are as true now as they were then. Golden memories of sounds and scents of the countryside are mine, too. The rustle of ripe wheat blowing in the warm summer breeze and the heady perfume of honeysuckle which grew in profusion along the hedgerows. Wild roses pure and sweet sprinkled with early morning dew. Meadow mushrooms just waiting to be gathered and the evening song of the nightingale. Those treasures and many more I took for granted then, but cherish now.

My parents worked very hard, and we had few luxuries, but we were happy; we had so much to enjoy.

CHAPTER
TWO

Mollie was my cousin whose mother had died just after she was born. My mother had cared for her since her birth, so she was more like a little sister to me. At the time we moved to Pengelly, she was almost a year old. Her father, Arnold (always my favourite uncle), was my mother's brother.

The year was 1921. Just why we went to live in such a remote part of Essex I have no idea, but I rather think it was because the house was big enough for Uncle Arnold and Mollie to make their home with us.

My parents were Londoners and had lived in Earlsfield since their marriage. They had always had a longing for the country life, so I imagine this was the opportunity they had been waiting for.

The house was about two and a half miles from Rayleigh Station and was approached by a cart track which turned off the Hullbridge Road. It was quite alone in the middle of a field; in fact, one had to follow the cart track through a field to reach the one in which the house stood. Beyond, a few cottages were scattered, and in these lived our nearest neighbours. I have often wondered why anyone would have chosen such an isolated spot to build a house like Pengelly.

It was double fronted with a red-tiled roof and white pebbledash walls. A balcony across the front of the house was supported by carved pillars, which were painted white. Underneath was a veranda, large enough for rustic type armchairs to be placed each side of the front door. A stained-glass panel in the door was matched with the small panes at the top of the large bay windows. After we had lived there for a short while, my father placed long boxes of geraniums, blue lobelia and various trailing plants along the balcony. The white walls were a perfect background for the scarlet and blue blossoms and lush green fronds which hung down through the balustrade.

Built onto one of the side walls was a very large lean-to greenhouse, and, on the other, there was an archway covered with pink Dorothy Perkins roses. This led to a gate at the side of the garden. The main gate at the front was painted white and had a hedge each side.

It was a lovely house, and people strolling across the fields on a summer's day would stop to admire it and wonder, I am sure, why anyone took so much trouble with the garden when most of the time there was no-one around to see it, except of course the family. Dad loved his garden and spent all his spare time working in it. The flower beds were a profusion of roses, fuchsias, irises and masses of other plants too numerous to mention.

We had a large lawn in front of the archway, and there, Uncle Arnold made us a swing. He hated gardening just about as much as Dad loved it, but he was a useful handyman and coped with a lot of repairs around the house and garden.

The back door opened onto a wide concrete yard next to the pump house. A pump house was considered a very sophisticated amenity at a time when most families around our area were drawing water from a well with a bucket and rope. We pumped ours into large enamel jugs, which were taken into the kitchen. Trenches had been dug in the fields to collect water as it drained from the land. Then it flowed into smaller trenches in our garden. These contained a series of filters through which the water passed on its way to the well. By this time, it was crystal clear, but we were never allowed to drink it until it had been boiled.

Across the yard was an outhouse. This boasted a small kitchen range with an oven. There was also a round, brick fireplace. On top of this was a large concrete container for the copper. The copper was like an enormous pudding basin with a wooden lid. My mother lit the fire underneath, and that was how we obtained hot water for baths and washing. In the corner was a storeroom; we used this for corn and poultry foods.

Snuggling coyly against the outhouse was what was politely called the "closet". This was the lavatory, which was surrounded with climbing roses, lilac and other shrubs. I always found it a delightful place in summer when it smelled sweetly of roses and lilac. In winter, I thought it the coldest place on earth. The lavatory seat was like a wooden bench with a hole cut in it and the front was boarded to conceal a real lavatory pan. In the corner stood jugs of water to which had been added Jeyes Fluid. We had to pour this down the lavatory each time we used it. One jug was quite small (for the children to lift), so there was no excuse for not doing so.

We had cesspool drainage, and one of my father's more unpleasant tasks was to pump it from the sump after it had been treated. It was then used as fertiliser on the garden. He tried to do this when the wind was strong enough to disperse the offensive stink this chore produced. The family name for this job was "dealing with the eckerpoosey".

Our garden at the back of the house was about one hundred yards long. On one side was an orchard and on the other a vegetable plot. We had another well at the bottom of the garden, which was securely covered with a strong lid. In the meadow beyond were sheds and barns near which was a kennel which housed a large dog. We took him over with the house. He was (we were told) a cross between an Airedale and a Retriever. Anyway, the result was a large black dog with long, soft, curly hair. The unfortunate animal had spent most of his life chained to the kennel and was reputed to be very fierce, mainly I suspect on account of his loud bark. We moved him into the house with us and found him to be very gentle. He became my friend and protector.

We had taken our cat, Smut, with us to Pengelly, and although he and Rover never became friends, they tolerated each other with a chilly indifference.

Dad and Uncle Arnold both worked in London, so each day they cycled to Rayleigh Station, left their bicycles there and continued their journey by train. They enjoyed their ride to the station in the summer, but in winter it was a very different story. The roads they travelled had no lights and were flanked by deep ditches. Their bicycles were equipped with oil lamps, which only sufficed to warn other travellers of their approach. During winter they left home before daylight and returned after dark. Later on, they had battery lamps which were a big improvement, but it was still a hazardous journey in a howling gale or on ice-covered roads.

I had never really noticed the pear tree opposite the back door; then one sunny morning, there it was, almost as high as the house, clothed in a froth of white blossom. Suddenly, I was aware of its beauty. I ran to it and encircled the trunk with my arms and gazed up at this sweet-scented cloud above me. Beyond the tree was a sea of forget-me-nots. Wall flowers were bobbing in the breeze filling the air with their soft velvety perfume.

That was the day I fell in love with flowers, with sunshine, with country smells and all things bright and beautiful.

CHAPTER
THREE

Before I go further, I must tell you about my family. Dad was of medium height, sturdily built without an ounce of fat. Wiry is probably an apt description. His unruly wavy hair was dark brown and his twinkling eyes bright blue. He was clean-shaven and his face always had a healthy, ruddy glow. Indeed, he was a very healthy man. Apart from the odd cold, I cannot remember his ever being ill. He was a wonderful teller of bedtime stories, and every evening I would sit on his lap by the kitchen fire and listen to the latest adventures of a little boy called Harry. He would always leave off just when something exiting was about to happen, so that I could anticipate the next episode. In his own unconventional way, he was deeply religious, believing that one should live a good life, not just talk about it. I never heard him use coarse language, and he always tried to see the best in people. He was also a romantic; he loved music and works of art, and birthdays and anniversaries were always remembered and celebrated.

Mum was a petite figure, certainly no taller than five feet two inches. Her long, almost-black hair was straight and shiny, coiled in a bun on the nape of her neck. She had large, smoky-blue eyes, fringed with black lashes, and her complexion was all her own. She considered Lifebouy soap and water were sufficient to keep her skin clean and fresh and would say frequently, "Nothing would induce me to put that muck on my face", when reading advertisements extolling the virtues of cosmetics, which she thought in bad taste. She was practical, capable and quick of movement and could be relied upon in any emergency. Although her demeanour was cool and calm, she had great depths of feeling for anyone in trouble.

Photographs taken when I was very small told me that I had very dark wavy hair, which hung in ringlets. I was slight of frame but quite robust, and I had inherited my mother's eyes.

Uncle Arnold was a tall, thin man. His hair was black and straight, and he wore it brushed back. Sometimes he had a fine black moustache, then he would get "fed-up" with it and shave it off, only to grow it again because his face looked bare without it. His eyes were like my mother's. When I sat on his shoulders as he walked down the garden path, I felt as high as the tallest tree.

I don't remember very much about Mollie before she was able to play with me. I used to notice her being fed, bathed and put in her pram, and that's about all. When she was about two years old, I became aware of her as a person. Her hair was brown and straight, and she had a fringe. Mollie was sturdy and cuddly and always smiling.

Because we lived in such a remote part of Essex, I seldom had any contact with other people during my early years. I can remember being wheeled in my pushchair to the shops in the village or visiting one of the cottages in the vicinity, but, apart from that, my time was spent almost entirely at Pengelly, which is probably why I remember so much; there were no distractions. My whole life centred around my parents, and the daily events absorbed me totally. I was loved, indulged and protected, and in return was expected to behave properly as befitted a little girl in those days.

CHAPTER
FOUR

After we had lived at Pengelly for a couple of years, Uncle Arnold brought a lady to see us. He told me to call her Auntie Madge. Young as I was, I still noticed that she had pretty, dark, curly hair and very dark-brown eyes. I had never seen such eyes before — everyone in my little world had blue. I thought they were beautiful, but most of all I envied her her dimples. I thought I would like to grow some, so I walked around with the forefinger of each hand pressed into my cheeks. My mother asked me what I was doing, and when I told her, she said, "You either have them or you don't; you can't make them. Anyway, you have one in your chin."

I looked in the mirror. So I had!

It is strange that this meeting with Auntie Madge is so clear in my mind, because I have absolutely no recollection of the day she and Uncle Arnold were married. It may have been because it was a quiet wedding, as she had no family. When I was old enough to understand, she told me that her parents had died when she was very young, and she and her brother had gone to live in an orphanage. Later, her brother had been killed in the war, and she was quite alone in the world when she met Uncle Arnold. Anyway, I woke one morning to find Mollie had a mummy and I had an auntie.

There was plenty of room at Pengelly for them to have their own rooms, and they lived with us for a while. Mollie and I had been brought up like sisters, so this was an ideal arrangement to give her time to adjust to her new mother, without depriving her of my mother's care completely while doing so. It was a happy arrangement for all concerned.

A few months later, in fact the following March, just after Dad had carried me up to bed and tucked me in, I heard strange voices in the hall below.

"Who are you, and why are you here?" I wondered. "I'll ask Mummy in the morning," I decided.

I didn't have to ask, because Dad came to my room very early and helped me dress, saying he had something very exciting to show me. He carried me along the landing to their bedroom. Mummy was still in bed, leaning back against the pillows. She was holding a baby!

"Come and see your baby brother," she said. I felt very shy and couldn't think what to say. I had only been there for a couple of minutes, when a lady in a stiff white cap and apron came in and hustled us out of the bedroom. I went downstairs with Daddy to have breakfast. Before he went to work, he told me I must be a good girl and do as the nurse told me. Soon after he left the house, nurse found my hat and coat and put them on me.

"Take your doll and doll's pram, and go and play in the garden," she said.

It was a miserable, cold day. A strong, chill wind was blowing, and I stood gazing forlornly through the kitchen window at the glowing fire and wishing I could go inside. Mummy never made me play outside when it was cold. I was desolate. Mummy had a new baby; Daddy had gone to work, and one-one loved me. My throat felt tight, and tears were welling in my eyes. Then Auntie Madge came and found me and told me to come and play with Mollie. Oh, how lovely it was to be wanted. Soon I was warm and quite pleased about the baby.

In those days, babies were usually born at home, and a nurse came and stayed for a couple of weeks while the mother rested in bed. Our nurse was a harridan, and I kept out of her sight as much as possible. I was allowed into my Mother's bedroom for only five minutes each evening to say "good night" to her. How I missed my Mum's presence and the comfort she gave me. I think Dad was just as relieved to see nurse go as I was. The day she left, we had a celebration game of "horses". I rode on Dad's shoulders all round the kitchen, up the stairs, along the landing and back again, and no one told me to be quiet. I was allowed to see my baby brother have his bath and was very concerned to know why he had that "big blister".

"That's because he is a little boy," my Mother told me.

"Oh," I said.

It seemed no time at all before my brother was smiling at me, and soon he was sitting up in his pram. He was chubby and golden haired, and I felt quite proud of him. He was christened Robert after my Father, but we always called him Bobby.

CHAPTER
FIVE

My Mother thought it would be a good idea if we kept some chickens. What could be nicer than freshly-laid eggs? We had several sheds at the bottom of the garden which could be made into suitable houses for them. Perches were made for them to roost, and nest boxes were installed along the sides. It was my job to fill them with straw. Rolls of wire netting were purchased, and a sizeable run was made around the sheds. We bought a dozen Rhode Island Red pullets, and Mr Gutteridge, who lived in a little white cottage in the meadow across the way, gave us a young cockerel of the same breed. He grew to be a magnificent bird. He wore his red comb like a crown. His bronze plumage was sleek, and his elegant tail feathers glistened blue and green, purple and black. He strutted around his new domain and became very self important and aggressive.

I remember the day of the first egg well. A cackling hen announced its arrival. Mum entered the run, and as she approached the shed, the rooster charged at her with his feathers standing on end. She flapped her apron at him, dived into the shed, found the egg and dashed out again. Soon we were getting eggs every day and collecting them became a battle of wits between

Mum and the cockerel. She found the best thing to do was take a jug of water with her when she entered the run and throw some at him if he got too close.

I had heard my parents talking about the recent war and noticed that whenever they talked of fighting, the Kaiser's name was mentioned. So, although I didn't understand who the Kaiser was, I suggested that, since the cockerel was always fighting, we should call him Kaiser. My parents and Uncle Arnold threw back their heads and laughed and made comments like, "Out of the mouths of babes". Anyway, Kaiser he became, and all agreed we couldn't have found a better name for him.

Soon, splashing him with water had little effect. In fact, he not only became immune to it, it actually seemed to enrage him further, and he became a fury of beak and claws. It was decided that he would have to be removed from the run whilst the hens were laying. But how to do it? Mr Gutteridge came over one evening, and when it grew darker, he peered into the gloom of the chicken house and located Kaiser, then he entered with a sack which he threw over the roosting bird. He bundled him up into it and bore him under his arm to an adjacent shed, where he had his own run alongside the hens. He occasionally returned to them by flying over the top, or by pushing up the wire netting. Having been shown how to deal with him, Dad became quite an expert at returning him to his own quarters. This manoeuvre was always accompanied by such a cacophony of squawks, that I dissolved into a state of helpless laughter.

16

Eventually we had about fifty or sixty hens, and Kaiser remained monarch. My Mother became a very successful breeder of Rhode Island Reds, and her chicks were always in demand. Sometimes, she would even supply a clutch of fertile eggs, if someone had a broody hen.

Having done so well with chickens, she thought it would be interesting to have some ducks as well. Aylesbury ducks would be very nice, she decided. So a small pond was made for them in the meadow just outside the garden. Although it was only twenty feet long by twelve feet wide, it took hours of digging. The excavated earth was banked up round the sides leaving access for the ducks at one end; this was a precaution against anyone falling in whilst walking in the dark. Gradually, it filled with water, and when the ducks arrived, it was ready for them. They became very tame and greeted us with enthusiastic quacks at feeding time.

One morning, I went with Mum to feed the chickens and ducks, and when this was done, she said, "I have a surprise for you." She opened the door of the barn, and there was Katy! She was a brindled, coffee-coloured goat, with a fine pair of horns and slanting topaz eyes. Our admiration for each other seemed to be mutual, and we became great friends. I would take hold of one of her horns, and we would wander around the field at the side of the house, where she found the sweetest clover. She was very playful and would prance about, gently butting me, until I sat down abruptly. Katy cropped the grass around the chicken house and in the orchard. This was a great help in keeping the place tidy.

Her capacity for food was astonishing, and she dealt quickly with thistles and nettles, too. Beside the barn, there was a large patch of stinging nettles to be cleared, but unfortunately they had grown up through some rolls of barbed wire, so Katy couldn't deal with those. Dad decided he would have to make a start on it, and whilst pondering on the best way to go about it, bent over to light his pipe, shielding the flame from the wind. Katy found this posture irresistible, and he suddenly found himself butted head first into the nettles. His hands and face were stung by nettles, and his hands were scratched by the wire, too. To make matters worse, his favourite pipe was lost in the tangled mess.

"Goodness what have you done?" asked my Mother as we entered the kitchen. Dad told her exactly what had happened, and, in no uncertain terms, what he thought of the goat. I kept pointing out that she was only playing, but he didn't seem to be listening.

Mum bathed Dads wounds and rubbed dock leaves on his nettle stings. I saw her lips twitching, as she tried not to laugh at the indignity he had suffered. Then his eyes meet hers, and he gave a sheepish smile. Suddenly they were both laughing till the tears ran down their faces.

"I do believe that goat has a sense of humour," chuckled Dad.

I didn't know what he meant, but I did know Katy was forgiven.

CHAPTER
SIX

One day, we went to Wickford Market and bought some young rabbits, and they were housed in a large hutch in the orchard. I loved the little creatures, and in my efforts to stroke them, I crawled right into the hutch. It was a windy day, and the door slammed behind me. I tried to poke my fingers through the wire, but they were too short to reach the catch. I called and called though no one could hear me. I was sure I would be forgotten and have to spend the night in the rabbit hutch. Of cause my parents were running all over the place trying to find me, never dreaming I was imprisoned in such an unlikely place. Their calls of, "Where are you?" were drowned by my wails of self-pity. I couldn't understand why they laughed when they found me.

"Never mind," said Dad. "Come and help me get some water from the bottom well."

When we needed water for baths or for Mum to do the washing, Dad had to draw it from the bottom well, as the well in the pump house supplied only enough for cooking and general household use.

I was very frightened of the bottom well. It was so deep, dark and narrow. I would hold my Father's jacket, thinking my puny efforts would prevent him falling in as he hauled the bucket to the top with a length of rope. He had to do this many times to fill the water wagon. Then he had to wheel it to the outhouse and empty it in the copper. Two large baths also had to be filled. This meant two more trips to the well. He also drew enough water to top up the two water butts, so that there was a supply of water for Mum to use during the week. He did this every Sunday.

In the summer, we had our baths in the outhouse, but in the winter, we had them in front of the fire in the kitchen. Towels hung warming on the fireguard, and how I enjoyed the delicious comfort of being enfolded by the soft warmth of them.

Actually, we had a spacious bathroom upstairs, which had a bath and washbasin with taps! But alas no water pipes. I suppose this was done in anticipation of a main water supply at a later date, but it was never available while we lived there. The bathroom was of no use at all. My Mother cleaned it once a week, but apart from that no one ever went in there.

CHAPTER
SEVEN

When Mollie was old enough, we spent many happy hours wandering around the fields, exploring the hedgerows. Sometimes, when picking wild flowers, we would come cross a lizard or a large hairy caterpillar. On several occasions, we found a nest of field mice with their pink "jelly-baby" young. Once or twice an agitated partridge fluttered into the air, calling "crikcrik", as we came too close to her nest. We would peep quickly at the olive green eggs, and once we saw the newly hatched young, which resembled our Rhode Island Red chicks. We always withdrew quickly and the bird would return. I suppose our parents had told us not to touch the nests, because we grew up with a very protective attitude to all wildlife.

The only creature my Mother detested was the stoat. It would burrow into the chicken houses and kill the sleeping bird by leaping at its throat, then try to drag it down its burrow, but the bulk of the bird's body would prevent it. I can remember my Mother following a trail of blood to the corner of the shed, where she found the body of a hen sticking up out of a hole with it's head chewed off. The only solution was to concrete the ground on which the sheds stood. The previous foundation was crumbling, and the stoat seemed instinctively to know the week spot.

Hawks were another hazard. They would swoop to the ground and snatch young chicks or ducklings, and we had to ensure that their runs were covered with wire netting. On occasions, I had seen them hover high in the sky, then plunge like a falling stone. Scarcely had they touched the ground than they were up again bearing aloft their luckless victim. Sometimes, I saw Kestrels snatch young wild rabbits, and I felt sick at the sight of them being borne away.

It was a mystery to me that every mole I saw was dead. It was a beautiful little creature, clad in a velvet black suit, with minute paws like little pink hands. I used to carry them tenderly into the house and ask Mother what the matter was with them and why they had died. No one could ever answer my questions.

Nearby was a large natural pond, and we often went there with our parents for a walk on a summer evening. Dragonflies hovered above the pond, their iridescent reds, greens and blues reflected in the water beneath them. We used to sit quietly, watching the moorhens and kingfishers. Kingfishers are the most beautiful of birds. They dart in flight, a flash of blue, quicker than the eye can follow.

Rover loved to swim in that pond and needed no encouragement to retrieve a stick thrown into the water.

As we walked back across the field at dusk, bats would swoop and whirl about us. Rustling sounds in the hedgerows told us that the wild creatures were settling down for the night, or nocturnal ones starting on their forage for food.

As we approached Pengelly, we could view how the brilliant sunset had painted its white walls pink. The trees in the orchard would be red and gold and the barn would be changed from black to russet. When we arrived at the house and turned to face the sunset, the trees were silhouetted black against the orange sky, their branches reaching up as if to embrace the night.

Such were the wonders of my childhood.

CHAPTER
EIGHT

Uncle Arnold came home from work one evening and told us he had heard about a house to let, so we all went along to have a look at it. It was only a short distance from Rayleigh Station, which would be more convenient for him. The house was exactly what they were looking for, so they decided to take it. I missed Mollie very much after they moved, even though we still saw each other quite often, since we had to pass their house every time we went to the village, as Rayliegh was called locally.

Bobby was still too young to play with me, but I had Rover, Katy and Smut for companions. I soon found Smut a very willing "baby"; I dressed him in my doll's clothes, wrapped him in a shawl and put him in my doll's pram. Then off we would go for a walk. He actually seemed to enjoy it and never made any attempt to escape from me or the pram. In fact, he would rub his sides against my legs, almost asking me to get on with the game. Sometimes I would wheel him across the field to the road to wait for Dad when he returned from London. I know everyone was surprised and amused that my "doll" was a black cat with green eyes, and they almost choked with mirth to see him lying there with a doll's dummy in his mouth. I found him a much more interesting "baby" than a doll. Our games continued for several years, and when Bobby was old enough, he joined me, too. He was "Father", and I was "Mother", and we took our baby for walks to visit our friends in the cottages nearby. We became a quite well known trio.

But there was another side to Smut's character. He was a hunter! He hunted anything that moved and would kill his prey, carry it home and deposit it on the doormat, almost as though he was bringing a gift. He hunted for pleasure, not because he was hungry. Birds, rats, mice and once a rabbit almost as big as himself, he brought into the kitchen. Even our chicks and ducklings fell victim to his attacks. Of course we employed every possible means of safeguarding them. But still an odd one would squeeze through the wire mesh. Smut even learned to claw at the wire netting until he had loosened it enough to crawl underneath. He became such a menace that we had to make a special run on a wooden base for the chicks. While this was being done Smut had to be kept indoors for a few days, so that the chicks could be let out for a while in their old run. We shut him upstairs in one of the unused bedrooms and were astonished to see him walking towards us five minutes later. He had jumped down from the window, which was a height of fifteen feet. He was taken back and the window closed.

On the day the new run was finished, Mum said I could go and let Smut out. I ran indoors, up the stairs and along the landing, flung open the door calling,

"Come on, Smutty", but he wasn't in the room! The window and door were both shut, but there was no sign of him. In a panic, I rushed back to my Mother, who returned to the bedroom with me, saying, "Don't be silly; he must be there." But he wasn't! The food we had left him had been eaten, and the saucer of milk was empty. Then Mum noticed a patch of soot in the hearth. She called, "Smut, come along," and the answer was a plaintive miaow. He had tried to escape by way of the chimney. It took some time to entice him down, and I was relieved to see him. I hugged him to me and ended up looking almost as black as he was.

Now that the chicks were safe, he was free again. Kaiser was sufficient deterrent to prevent him attacking the hens, and the ducks always took to the water at his approach, so the problem was solved. I am sorry to say the wild creatures were not so fortunate, but one thing in his favour was the fact that he killed instantly. He never played with his victims as some cats do. One pounce and it was all over. After all, we were pleased when he caught rats or mice in the barn, so how could we, in fairness, censure him for killing birds?

CHAPTER
NINE

We went to see Mrs Gutteridge one afternoon. She owned a little brown and white mongrel called Patsy, and she'd had five puppies. I was enchanted. I had never seen a puppy before. My heart sang when Mrs Gutteridge said, "Come back in three weeks, and you can have one. They are too tiny to leave their mother yet." This was all prearranged between my mother and Mrs Gutteridge, but I hadn't been told.

How slowly the time went. I think I must have driven my parents mad with my incessant demands of, "How much longer?"

The day eventually came when I could have my puppy. I felt sick with excitement. It was a sparkling morning, the sunlight making the dew on the grass look like a million diamonds. A skylark soared in the sky, singing its happiness. Such a summer sound. The whole of the countryside knew it was a special day and shared my joy.

We arrived at the little white cottage. Now I could have my puppy. But how would I choose? They were all delightful. There were two exactly alike, and I picked one of them. There was a whispered conversation between Mum and Mrs Gutteridge. The one I had chosen was a little girl puppy. Mum thought Rover would rather have a boy to play with. It was fortunate that the identical one was a boy. I couldn't imagine how they knew. Puppies were puppies and dogs were dogs as far as I understood. Until that moment, I hadn't realised animals were male and female just like people.

"I'll call him Jackie," I said, and it was agreed that it was a very good name for him. His back was dark brown, shading to tan on his head and flanks, and he had a little tuft of hair each side of his mouth. I scooped him up in my arms, pressing my face against his. I could smell the sweetness of his breath as he yawned, and I squeezed the loose folds of his skin between my fingers and glowed with love for him. I wanted to carry him all the way home, but my arms were aching, so I had to give him to Mummy. She carried him the rest of the way, and when we went into the kitchen, she put him down on the floor and said to Rover, "There you are, a new friend for you." Rover welcomed him like an indulgent uncle, wagging his tail and sniffing him all over. Smut gave a cold stare and, tail erect, strode haughtily into the garden. I went to fetch Katy to meet him, and when she came to the door, she lowered her head to look at him, and, curiosity satisfied, she ambled away.

We knew Jackie had been accepted.

CHAPTER
TEN

Living as we did deep in the heart of the county, we were never short of summer visitors. Grandparents, uncles, aunts and cousins all came to spend their holidays with us. Of course, I had my favourites and have very happy memories of their visits. They all lived in or around London, so a week or two in our peaceful countryside was a great pleasure for them.

Our most faithful visitors were Auntie Beatie and her friend, Miss Brooker. Auntie Beatie was my father's sister, a widow whose husband had died of his war wounds. Miss Brooker's young man had been killed in battle just before the war ended. We always called her Auntie Brook.

They came to see us in winter as well as summer, so they were special. Sometimes they would arrive drenched to the skin, having walked from the station through pitch-black lanes in pouring rain. If anyone was coming our way with a pony and trap, they would be lucky and get a lift. Even then they had to stumble along the cart track to the house. Finally, gusts of wind would almost lift them off their feet, as they opened the door and burst into the kitchen. Amidst splutters of laughter, they would peel off their wet macs, raindrops running down their faces.

They both worked in one of the large stores in the West End of London, and, though times were hard for them, they never came without a little present for us children. I remember in particular the hair ribbons they gave me, especially the shot-silk ones. They changed from green to gold or pink to mauve as I moved my head. I thought they were beautiful and tossed my curls so that everyone would notice them. I didn't realise the smiles they gave were of amusement and not admiration as I had hoped.

I remember one summer's evening, when they were spending a weekend with us, we walked to Hullbridge and went down to the river Crouch to watch the barges go by. The dull red sails were reflected in the water as they glided slowly along. The river traffic was very busy at high tide, and I found it fascinating to watch the precision of the oars as the ferrymen rowed their boats across the water from Woodham Ferrars.

Down by the waterfront was a tiny sweet shop, and for a halfpenny we could buy all sorts of childish delights. A sugar egg was my favourite. It was hollow and moulded over rice paper. Inside, wrapped in greaseproof paper, was a little gift. Oh the excitement and joy of anticipation. Would it be a ring or a necklace, a badge or lucky charm?

A halfpenny would also buy a liquorice pipe and a little packet of liquorice "bootlaces" or a "Bonker Bar", which was a delicious brittle coffee flavoured toffee. If we only had a farthing to spend, we could buy some aniseed balls or a sugar stick.

Having spent the halfpenny allowed on this occasion, we were strolling homewards when we heard a buzzing, droning sound high in the sky.

"An aeroplane," cried Daddy, and all the grown-ups shaded their eyes against the glare of the sun and gazed into the clear blue sky. "There it is," he shouted. "Look Doris, look, an aeroplane. You are a lucky girl to see that."

I looked at a small object in the sky. I wasn't impressed. It just looked like a bird.

"It's really quite big; it only looks small because it's so far away," said Dad. "There is a man in it making it fly."

Now I was interested.

"How does he make it fly?" I wanted to know, and, "Why did he go up there?" followed by, "But what for?"

I think they all began to wish I hadn't seen it.

When we arrived home, I walked down the garden and climbed a pair of steps which were leaning against one of the sheds and scrambled onto the roof. I held my arms at my sides like an aeroplane and jumped, expecting to glide gracefully through the air. The result was a disaster: cuts and grazes on my knees, and my teeth went through my lower lip. I rushed into the house, bellowing with rage and pain and disappointment. My wounds were bathed, and gradually my sobs subsided. I hiccuped that I only wanted to fly.

"You must never climb on the sheds again," said Mummy, kissing me better. "You are lucky you are not badly hurt."

Not badly hurt! I was hurting everywhere! Despite the mishap, I still ran out to look every time I heard an aeroplane.

CHAPTER
ELEVEN

In front of the house was a cornfield, and there was another one along the side by the orchard. I loved to watch the ploughing and sowing of corn in the spring and to see fresh, green spikes appear through the dull, brown earth. Before long, it was as tall as me, and soon it began to change from green to gold. Scarlet poppies and white dog-daisies were scattered here and there amidst the corn, and I walked around the edge of the field gathering little posies to give to Mum. The dry corn stalks whispered in the wind, and grasshoppers chirruped. Bees buzzed in the clover, while swallows swooped over me. I could feel the warmth of the sun and the soft fresh air caressing my bare arms and legs. The happiness I felt deep inside me was almost too much to be locked inside my small frame.

When the time came for the corn to be harvested, I spent hours by the garden gate watching the magnificent Shire horses pulling the cutting machines around the field, working from the outer edges towards the middle. The horses always seemed to know exactly where to go. When they reached the corners, they lifted their great hairy feet, crossing them daintily like a dancer, as they swung the machine around.

Mum used to take the men jugs of tea and freshly baked cakes.

"They must be dying for a cup of tea," she would say.

They called me "little darlin'" and "princess" and teased me saying, "Can I have one of your curls?" I thoroughly enjoyed all the attention.

When only a smallish square of uncut corn remained, Mum always found some reason for getting me into the house. I didn't realise that all the wild rabbits had withdrawn into the middle of the field, seeking refuge from the blades. They made a dash for freedom as their cover became smaller and smaller, and the men stood ready to shoot them as they ran. Many families had rabbit stew that night!

When all the corn was cut, tied into sheaves and stacked, it looked very neat and tidy. The next day, three men would come along with a horse and wagon. One would lead the horse from stack to stack, while another would pick up a sheaf with a pitchfork and toss it in to the man on the wagon, who placed it carefully in position so that it could be piled high.

After this was done, we were allowed to go gleaning. We picked up all the stalks that had been missed, then cut off the ears of corn and put them into sacks and saved them for the chickens. At feeding time, we'd throw some into the run, and the birds would scratch busily with fussy side-kicking movements to pick out the grains of corn. The stalks provided extra straw for the nest boxes. When we had collected all we could, our chickens were permitted into the field to eat the grains that had fallen. Nothing was wasted.

It was on one such occasion that Kaiser really disgraced us. A young lad used to bring us milk from his father's farm. He carried it in two large cans and measured it with a ladle into our jugs. He was about to open our gate when Kaiser saw him and tore across the field, a whirlwind of fury. He leapt on his shoulders and started pecking his head (which was fortunately covered by a soft cap) and beating his wings against him. The poor lad dropped the cans, and the milk spilt onto the dry earth and disappeared. My Mother was aghast; she beat off the bird with her broom, dragged Willie inside, set him down in the kitchen and gave him a cup of tea. She paid for all the lost milk and said she would keep Kaiser locked up until after he called in future.

The next morning the hens were let out into the field again, but Kaiser was left in his run. My Mother happened to glance out of the window and there was the postman running as fast as his legs would carry him, giving quick desperate glances over his shoulder. Close behind was Kaiser, hurtling along, half flying, half running. Mum grabbed a broom and ran out of the door to do battle again. She apologised to the postman and explained that she had left the bird in his run. She found out later that he had pushed against the wire netting until one of the pegs holding it down had been loosened, then he'd squeezed himself underneath it and escaped.

The morning after that, he flew out over the wire. One of our farmer friends advised clipping his wings, and that certainly worked for a while.

The postman took to blowing a whistle before he approached the house; this was to give us warning of his arrival, so that we could ensure that he was not attacked again. He was a surly individual and not very well liked. His dash across our field had been witnessed by a couple of farm labourers and related to all their friends. The joke about his "fast delivery" lasted a very long time.

Bread was delivered to the house, as well as groceries, meat, poultry foods, coal and paraffin. It says a great deal for the quality of service supplied by tradesmen in those days, when one considers the distance between each house.

Our baker's bread was home-made and delicious. He brought it in a horse-drawn van. The shelves inside were well stocked with loaves of every shape and size.

The "Oilman" delivered things such as black lead, hearthstone, carbolic and soap, as well as paraffin. Black lead was used to polish the kitchen range and fireplaces, hearthstone for whitening the steps, hearths and the floor of the pump house. There was quite an art to applying hearthstone, which had to be rubbed all over the freshly washed, and still wet, step or hearth. When it dried, it was a dazzling white.

The first washing powder my Mother used was "Hudsons". It was sold in little brick-shaped bags. After years of washing clothes with hard soap and soda using a scrubbing board, she thought it very up-to-date to have a quick dissolving powder. She still had to use a brush and scrubbing board though.

CHAPTER
TWELVE

During the winter, we lived in the kitchen. The parlour was an enormous room and took a great deal of heating. We had to light a fire hours before the room was needed, so in winter we used it only at Christmas. In summer, it was a haven from the heat.

The kitchen was always cosy. In front of the range was a shiny brass fireguard, which glinted gold and red in the firelight. Kettles of water were always on the hob, and all the cooking was done on the hotplate or in the oven.

The furniture was slightly shabby but comfortable, and the room made everybody feel welcome. It was the place where we all gathered — friends, family and neighbours alike — because it was homely. We had oil lamps for lighting and had to be careful that the lamp was not in direct line with the door, for when it was opened, the cold draught would crack the glass, and a broken lamp glass meant resorting to candles.

The entrance hall, leading from the front door, was impressive, with its dark green embossed wallpaper and white-painted skirting boards, doors and staircase. The staircase itself was wide, with brass stair rods holding the carpet in place.

My Mother had a tremendous area of lino to polish in the hall and sometimes asked us to help. I soon discovered the easiest way was to tie dusters over my feet and shuffle along. This led to sliding to and fro along the floor with great enthusiasm. I acquired a good sense of balance at an early age, and my young male cousins found I could compete very favourably when we made slides on the ice. I was even voted a good sport — for a girl!

CHAPTER
THIRTEEN

My Mother's parents lived in London, and Nanna's health had been causing concern for some time, so now, as Granddad had retired, they agreed to come and live with us, taking over the rooms which Uncle Arnold and Auntie Madge had occupied.

Granddad was a very upright gentleman with a fine moustache and thick grey hair. Nanna had silky grey hair worn in a bun. She always wore black, and her skirts swept the ground. Her blouses were severe in style but always trimmed with black lace. Having been born in County Cork, she spoke with a soft Irish accent. She had a very comfortable lap, and I remember thinking it was bigger than my Mother's. Sometimes she teased me by switching the words of the old nursery rhyme.

"What are little girls made of?" she would say. "Girls are made of snaps and snails and puppy dogs tails," and boys were made of "sugar and spice and all things nice."

I used to get quite upset, because I thought I was quite nice, really. This is about all I remember of Nanna, bar one other thing comes to mind. Granddad would pour them a glass of stout during the winter evenings, and Nanna would put the poker in the fire until it was red-hot, then plunge it into the beer. There would follow a hissing sound, and steam would rise from the glass.

"Ah that's better," they'd say, having taken a sip. It seemed such an odd thing to do, which is probably why I remember it.

The only other thing I recall is the smell of Sloan's liniment for Nanna's "Rheumatics".

It was just after Nanna and Granddad's arrival at Pengelly that Uncle Arnold and Mollie called to see us one Sunday morning. Mollie came running across the field calling excitedly, "I've got a baby brother, too. His name's Dennis." Everyone looked very pleased, and we were told he had very dark hair and took after his mother.

Mollie had come to stay with us for a while, so that Mum could take care of her while the nurse took care of Auntie Madge and the new baby. Mollie was tucked into bed with me that night, and it was lovely. We whispered together for a long time before going to sleep, telling each other all our secrets; and I told Mollie about going to school.

"I'll soon be old enough," I said, "when I'm five."

CHAPTER
FOURTEEN

With school days fast approaching, I had to learn to be self-reliant. I had been dressing myself for sometime, but still needed help with buttons and bows, like my vest, which tied with a ribbon at the neck, and a liberty bodice, which was like a waistcoat and buttoned down the front. Over this went my "combinations" which I hated! They were an all in one garment with a short sleeve and a short leg. They buttoned down the front but were divided just below the navel through to the waistline at the back, so that the legs separated to enable me to "spend a penny". Over these, I wore bloomers and a petticoat which tied at the neck and waist at the back. Finally I had to put on a dress or jumper and skirt. Dressing in the winter was a lengthy process for a little girl, and even little boys had their problems. They also wore the hated combinations and a liberty bodice.

I wore knee length boots during the winter and in spring and autumn, too, if we had rainy weather. My boots were made of soft black leather and were laced from the instep to the knee. At the top, the laces were looped round metal tags to prevent them slipping and were then tied in a bow. Oh, the frustration! The times

I'd lace the boots only to find I'd missed one of the eyelets and have to start all over again.

Summer was much easier. If it was very hot, I was allowed to wear just a dress and bloomers, if I was staying in the garden, otherwise I had to wear a dress, petticoat, bloomers and vest. I always had to be correctly dressed for going out.

At last, it was my fifth birthday. I now considered myself a big girl and felt very superior to the child who went to bed the night before. It was the first day of March, and thin bright sunlight was streaming through the parlour window. I lay on the rug by the fireplace and listened to the wind howling in the chimney, thinking about school. Then I got up and sat by the window and felt the warmth of the sun through the glass. Looking out of the window, I noticed some early daffodils in bloom, their heads tossing in the wind. In the sky, birds were being swept off course or held stationary, with flapping wings, in the grasp of the gale.

I would go to Hullbridge school after Easter, and Mum had promised to take me to the concert at the end of term so that I could investigate the school and see what a lovely time I would have.

The day arrived, and I went to the school with Nanna and Granddad, Mum and Bobby, all dressed in our best, to have my name put on the register and then to see the concert. We took our seats in the hall, which was really two rooms with a partition folded back against the wall, and I waited with baited breath. A lady came in, gave a little bow to the audience and started to play the piano.

When the curtains parted on the stage, little girls in all shapes and sizes rushed on merrily, prancing and tossing their curls. They carried garlands of paper flowers and were singing gaily, "I'm in the land of I don't know where, sleep is the driver who takes me there."

So repetitive were these words that they have remained indelibly printed in my mind.

I thought it was wonderful. If this was school, I couldn't wait to start. I remember vaguely that the boys also came on to do their turn. They were carrying large balls and boats, but they didn't have pretty dresses, so I looked around and absorbed the atmosphere. I could feel someone touching my hair and turned round to see a little boy. We smiled at each other, and he said, "Isn't your hair long?"

After the concert, I tried to stand up but found my head wouldn't come with my body. We discovered that the little boy had tied two of my ringlets together round the back of the chair. Of course he made a quick exit. My Mother had some difficulty in extricating me as the hair had become tangled, and her efforts were accompanied by squeaks of protest from me.

Granddad said, "He was just mischievous; they are not all like that."

I soon discovered that most of them were.

CHAPTER
FIFTEEN

When the time came for me to go to school, my Mother sat me on the carrier of her bike, and off we went. Nanna took care of Bobby in her absence. It was over two miles to school, and the wind was so cold and strong that Mum had quite a struggle to keep her balance.

The weather surprised me. I thought anything as important as my first day at school would have guaranteed a nice day.

Although I had passed the school when out walking and had attended the concert, it hadn't meant very much until that morning when it suddenly became my personal property. My school. It was quite a small building, with only three rooms — or four at most when the partition was pulled across. There were two cloakrooms — one for the boys, and one for the girls. The outside walls were sand coloured. I liked the shape of the roof and approved of the white steps as we entered through the large green doorway.

"Yes, I will like it here," I decided.

We arrived early, and I was daunted by the children who gathered round to have a look at the new girl. Within a few minutes, three other new girls joined us, and two small boys followed them. We stared at each other solemnly. Then the teacher came and said, "Say goodbye to your mothers children and come with me."

I gave my Mother a last appealing glance and toddled in with the other children.

"What's your name?" asked a little girl in red.

"Doris," I replied.

"Mines Miriam," she whispered. We held hands and went into the cloakroom together where we hung our hats, coats and satchels on pegs so low that even I could reach them. We had to take sandwiches to eat at lunchtime, so we all had to have a satchel or bag in which to leave them.

I asked one of the other new girls her name.

"Doris," she said.

"It's not."

"It is."

"It's not. My name's Doris."

I didn't like her. She didn't like me. We stood eyeing each other suspiciously. Until then, neither of us realised that several people could have the same name. That was our first lesson.

We went into our classroom. There was a blazing fire in the hearth with a high guard around it. It looked very welcoming. There were five long desks each accommodating five or six children. We were told to take our places on the front one. We had to slide along on our bottoms until we were all seated. I turned round and noticed that each form was bigger than the one in front and so were the children. This was the "infants" room where children remained until they were seven.

Each term, we moved back one row, to make room for the new intake of pupils, so the teacher had under her instruction children whose ages ranged from five to seven. Yet she taught us all exceedingly well.

When we left the "infants", we moved into the next room. Here children were taught until the age of fourteen, when they left school. The remaining room was used for cookery and domestic lessons for the girls and woodwork and handicrafts for the boys.

The lavatories were right across the other side of the playground, and only dire necessity made me make a dash for relief in pouring rain. Needless to say, the rain didn't help us contain ourselves.

The first week at school, we played with modelling clay, threaded beads or listened to stories. This gave us time to settle down and get to know each other. Then work began in earnest. By the end of the first term, I could say the alphabet forwards and backwards and write "the cat sat on the mat". By the time I was six and a half years old, I could read a newspaper. Of course I stumbled over long words and didn't understand their meaning anyway, but it says a lot for the method of teaching in those days. My parents put newspapers on a shelf where I couldn't reach them, as they were considered most unsuitable reading for a child. I read everything I could see: labels on jam jars, advertisements on hoarding's, signposts, even my mothers cookery books. Learning was so exciting.

It was a very happy school, and the eighty or so children who attended came from a radius of several miles. Some of the children came from Woodham Ferrers and were ferried across the river morning and afternoon in a rowboat. On occasions, a small brother or sister would be brought to school because "Mum's got another baby, and there's no one to look after him". It was quite common for six children of one family to be attending school at one time. Some of them came from desperately poor homes, living in wooden cottages that were little more than shacks. Most of the children were adequately, if poorly, dressed, but I particularly remember one small boy who came to school on a bitterly cold winter's day wearing heavy leather boots several sizes too large for him and no socks. He had only a shirt with a woollen scarf around his shoulders. He was always spotlessly clean, cheerful and uncomplaining.

When the weather was very cold, the teacher would put potatoes to bake in the ashes under the grate in the classroom. As we came out of school, she would hand them to the most needy children, "to keep your hands warm on the way home". The fact that they were eaten as soon as they were outside the school gate made no difference. This was obviously her intention and was accepted by the other pupils without question.

As soon as I became used to school, Mum took me as far as Watery Lane where I met other children, and we walked to school together. I loved the walk when the hedgerows were covered with hawthorn blossom or "May" as we called it. Later there were stitchwort stars covering the banks, and the scent of meadow sweet filled the air. We'd pick buttercups and make daisy chains, walking in shafts of sunlight that pierced the trees, dappling the road ahead.

The school summer holiday was known locally as the "pea picking holiday" because school closed to allow children to accompany their parents to the fields to gather the peas which were ready for marketing. Whole families would go along to help, to earn money, which in many cases was badly needed. The poverty of unemployment was dreadful, and casual labour rewarded with a pittance, but at least there would be enough money for food for a few weeks.

If I have given the impression that we were well to do, it would be untrue; my parents had to struggle to make ends meet. Dad was fortunate to have secure employment, so a regular income and careful management made us a rather privileged family in the area. I remember asking my mother, "Why can't we go pea picking?" It sounded such fun.

"Others have greater need of the money. It wouldn't be right," was her reply.

The summer holiday for me meant weeks of freedom, running through fields shoulder high with grass and dog daisies, gathering wild flowers and making them into garlands, romping with the dogs, watching baby chicks emerge from the shells and shaking earth off the newly dug potatoes, anticipating the flavour when they were cooked with a sprig of mint. The scent of sweet peas and roses — these were my riches, and I asked for nothing more.

CHAPTER
SIXTEEN

"We'll have a day at Southend tomorrow," Granddad said. "My treat."

I was thrilled to go to bed early that night. It would make the morning come quicker. The outing had been planned a few days ahead, but I hadn't been told before, because I would have become too excited.

The next morning we were up early, the chickens and ducks fed and Katy tied up with a stout rope in the field outside the garden. The dogs were exercised and shut in the house for the day. All was ready, so we set off: Nana, Granddad, Mummy, Bobby in his pushchair and me skipping along joyfully at their side. At the bottom of the field where it joined the road, Mr Pudney met us with his taxicab. This was a rare luxury and probably the only means by which Nanna could manage the trip. A walk across the field was as far as she could go.

When we arrived at Rayleigh station, Auntie Madge, Mollie and Dennis were waiting for us. We felt very sorry for our Dads, because they had to go to work and couldn't come with us.

The train roared into the station and, when it stopped, steam came hissing out in a most alarming manner. I hid behind Granddad, and Mollie hid behind her mother. Bobby and Dennis were just about to start crying when the noise stopped, and we were lifted into the train. We travelled so fast, the fields and houses were flashing by, and I listened to the train saying, "clunkety-clunk" all the way to Southend.

When we came out of the station, Granddad bought buckets and spades for each of us children, and we walked down the road that led to the sea. On our way there was a shop with green glass at the top of the windows, and when we went inside it was cool, green and dark. A most delicious smell of vanilla and strawberries pervaded the air. There were bottles of fizzy drinks on the shelves, and the grown-ups all agreed that a glass of lemonade would go down very well. The shopkeeper took down four bottles and held them one at a time just below the counter. There was a popping noise, and when he put them back on the counter the marbles which had been at the top of the bottle were now lying on the bottom. They poured the lemonade into their glasses, and I wondered how they put the marbles into the bottles, because the top wasn't big enough to get them out.

Granddad asked for ice creams for the children. What bliss, what ecstasy. They were made with real cream and fresh strawberries. I gazed at the confection with greedy eyes. Our tongues licked them delicately, flicking over the surface gently, to make them last as long as possible.

"Shall we go on the pier?" Granddad asked.

"Yes please," we all cried.

It was too far for Nanna to walk, so Granddad hired a chair for her to rest on until we came back.

I thought we would never reach the end. The boys were each in a pushchair, and I began to wish I was too. Mollie was trailing her wooden spade behind her, when it caught in a gap between the boards on which we were walking. It was snatched from her hand, and I watched it drop to the green sea below with a sort of sick dread. It was as though I was that spade falling to the depths below. Mollie and I gazed at each other wordlessly.

At the end of the pier was a big boat, and we were promised a trip on one when our brothers were a bit older. In the sea were huge jellyfish flopping against the wooden pillars which supported the pier.

We rode back to the beach on the pier's own train. It was much quicker than walking. Nanna had had a nice rest, so we went down to the beach and spent the rest of the day there. We made sandcastles and paddled in the sea. Then we had a picnic lunch and paddled again. Granddad put a handkerchief over his face and went to sleep, and I thought it was such a waste of a lovely day. I wanted it to go on forever. But all too soon it was time to go home.

When we arrived at Rayliegh station, we said goodbye to Auntie Madge, Mollie and Dennis, and Mr Pudney met us with the taxicab to take us home.

As we approached the house, Mum said, "Where's Katy?"

We ran forward and found her rope had been severed. Mum looked anxious, and I thought someone had stolen her.

"Oh my giddy aunt," gasped my mother, dashing off. We followed her, and there was Katy. She had chewed through the rope, eaten her way through the hedge and entered the garden, where she had devoured roses, fuchsias and all the other plants too. Her sides were bulging, and she was still eating.

We were given a hastily prepared meal and packed off to bed before Dad came home. How he reacted to the devastation, I never knew. It must have been heartbreaking — months of work wiped out in a few hours.

After that incident, Katy was always secured with a strong chain when we were not around to keep an eye on her.

CHAPTER
SEVENTEEN

I was playing in the field one Sunday morning when I saw Uncle Arnold come striding along the cart track. He waved to me, and I ran to meet him. He had a box under his arm, which he said was a surprise. He looked very pleased with himself.

We went into the kitchen, and he put the box down on the dresser.

"Well there it is," he said. "What we need now is an aerial. I have arranged for a pole to be delivered, so next weekend we should have it working."

"What is it?" I wanted to know.

"It's a crystal set," Uncle Arnold replied. "You'll know all about it soon."

During the week, the pole arrived, then we had to wait until Saturday before Uncle Arnold and Dad could do anything with it. They started by walking about thirty yards down the garden, where they stopped, looked back at the house and said, "that should do it." They dug a deep hole and dragged the thick end of the pole towards it. They fixed a long piece of wire to the top of it and four more pieces about halfway down. Then they put the thick end of the pole in the hole and huffed and puffed until they had raised it in a vertical position. Uncle Arnold held the pole up straight while Dad filled in the hole with the earth they had dug out. He rammed it down hard. Then they pegged the four pieces of wire into the ground some distance away to act as stakes. Having done this, they carefully unravelled the long piece of wire and carried it towards the house. Then Uncle Arnold climbed a ladder and fixed it to the roof, so that it was level with the top of the pole. The piece that was left hanging was passed through a small hole, which Dad made in the window frame, and attached to the "thing" on the dresser.

"Well now we've got the aerial up, let's see what happens," said Uncle Arnold, looking excited. There was an air of mystery about the whole project.

After a lot of fiddling with knobs, he told me to keep very quiet and put some things called earphones on his head. Then he turned the knobs again. He made me jump when he shouted, "I've got it." I couldn't see what he'd got, but Mum and Dad looked very impressed. They took turns to put on the earphones and said, "Isn't it amazing!" and "Marvellous". They thought it was very clever of Uncle Arnold to make a crystal set.

Now I was to have a go. Uncle Arnold put the earphones on my head. I didn't know what to expect.

"What can you hear?" asked Uncle Arnold with an indulgent smile.

"A funny noise?" I said hopefully.

"That's a man talking. You can hear him all the way from London," he said.

"Well he's quacking," I said.

"If you keep quite, you'll hear some music in a minute," Uncle told me. A faint, tinny sound crackled in my ear. It was most disappointing. Our gramophone was much better, especially when we played *Just a Song at Twilight* or *Pale Hands I love Beside the Shalimar*. That was lovely; but the crystal set had come to stay. A few years later, we had a loud speaker and I liked that. It was just as good as the gramophone.

CHAPTER
EIGHTEEN

At the beginning of September, I returned to school. A golden autumn brightened our walk in. Scuffling our feet through fallen leaves, stopping from time to time to pick up a beautiful bronze or red one to take to the teacher for 'Nature Study', or picking seeded heads of flowers, which had faded for an autumn "arrangement" in the classroom, added to the pleasure of those bright mornings.

Before we knew it, winter was upon us. Crisp frosty mornings when our breath hung mistily before us in the air. Sometimes a farmer would come along the road with a horse and empty cart. Then we were in luck. He would give us a lift. It was great fun. We sang to the rhythm of the horse's hooves, clip-clopping along the road.

Sometimes in very wet weather, we arrived at Watery Lane to find it flooded (its name was appropriate, and I suspect that was how it originated), then someone would be waiting with a horse and cart to carry the children across. The patient horses never seemed to mind plodding through the water. The only reward they expected was a sugar lump, and they would nuzzle our hands to see if we had brought our fare.

★ ★ ★

The following spring, Nanna became very ill. Her bed was brought downstairs to their living room, and she spent a lot of time resting on it. Sometimes she sat by the fire in her wicker armchair, but she didn't knit any more.

Bobby and I were playing Snakes and Ladders in the kitchen, because Mum was looking after Nanna and we had to be quiet. Auntie Madge and Uncle Arnold came to see us, bringing Mollie and Dennis with them. This was a lovely surprise, and we were very pleased to see them. Mollie and Dennis stayed in the kitchen and joined our game. After a while, Auntie Madge called me into the hall and said, "Doris you are the eldest, so I want you to take the others up to the spare bedroom and play there. You must be very quiet because Nanna is very ill and the doctor is coming."

This made me feel very subdued, but at the same time I felt very important. It was the first time in my life I had been asked to look after anybody. I collected my little flock and took them upstairs.

The spare bedroom had a high window, and a double bed was against the wall underneath it. I thought it would be a good idea if I read them a story. I was proud of the fact that I could struggle through a simple fairy tale.

Bobby started playing with the key in the lock.

"Bobby!" I said, but it was too late. There was a click, and the door was locked. I tried to turn the key back, but it was a faulty lock, and I couldn't move it. Mollie tried, Bobby tried and even little Dennis tried, all with no success. The boys started to cry, but I said, feeling very grown up, "Don't worry. My Daddy will be home soon, and he'll come and get us out when it's time for tea."

We played games, and I read to them for what seemed a very long time, and then Auntie Madge came to fetch us for tea. She tried the door, and I told her what had happened. She fetched Uncle Arnold. He told me to try and turn the key again, but I couldn't move it. He said, "Now listen; just be quiet. I'll get a ladder and try and get in through the window." Fortunately it was a sash window and slightly open at the top.

A few minutes later, I heard voices in the garden below. Standing on the bed, I could just see out of the window. Then I saw the top of the ladder appear. It came just about six inches above the windowsill. Dad had arrived home by this time, and as Uncle Arnold held the ladder to steady it, he climbed up to the window. As the window was open, he was able to slide the lower half up until there was a space at the bottom. The only way he could get through the narrow space was to dive headfirst onto the bed below. As he did so, his heels swung back and shattered the glass. He landed on the bed in a crumpled heap, pieces of glass falling all around him.

Just at that moment, Bobby fiddled with the key again. There was a click; he turned the handle, and the door was open.

A few days later, Nanna died. We were too young to understand death and were told that she had gone to heaven to be an angel. This satisfied us, because the

Bible stories told us heaven was a wonderful place to be.

On the day of the funeral, our friends at the farm looked after us. Mr Patmore took us to see the new calves, and we laughed when they sucked our fingers. I was allowed to hold a little squealing piglet. We went to see the cows being milked and were each given a glass of milk while it was still warm. For tea, we had home-made scones with cream from the dairy and strawberry jam. They were delicious. We had a lovely day and were quite unaware of the sad occasion it was for our parents.

For several weeks after Nanna died, I remember how I used to lie in the field looking up to heaven. High above the fluffy clouds, it was clear and blue and went on forever and ever. I thought it must be beautiful up there. I thought if I kept very still, Nanna might be able to see me when she looked down at Pengelly.

CHAPTER
NINETEEN

With the resilience of childhood and the arrival of long summer days, recent events soon faded from our minds. All around, foals, calves and piglets were arriving in abundance. The wild birds had fledglings in their nests. Our hens had their families of chicks and the ducklings were swimming on the pond. All the animals had babies. I asked Mum if I could get a baby dog for Rover and Jackie, and why hadn't they got a puppy.

"We have enough animals," my mother replied. I could not understand why Smut didn't have kittens either, and my Mother's reply hadn't answered my question.

At school, John Willis (whose nickname was know-it-all-Willis) kept telling us, "We've got a new calf" or, "Topsy had a foal last night". How I envied him. He was about thirteen years old and thought himself far superior to us seven-year-olds.

As if to grant me a wish, Katy produced twin kids. Oh happy day; now I had something to tell John Willis. When I saw him at school, I was determined to get my news in first, so I ran to him and said, "Katy's got two kids."

"Course she has," he replied with a supercilious sneer. "Our Billy goat — her didn't he?"

I was astonished. I didn't know what he was talking about, but I wasn't going to let him know that. I would ask Mum when I got home.

"Mummy what did John Willis' Billy goat do to Katy when he — her? He said that's why she had her kids," I asked at the first opportunity.

My mother's hand flew to her throat, and she looked quite ill. Her face went all red.

"You bad wicked girl," she said grabbing my hand and dragging me to the wash basin, where she liberally soaped a flannel. "I'm going to wash your mouth out with soap and water to make sure you never use that word again." After that, she stood me in the corner of the room, with my face to the wall. A door was in a convenient position to pull it back and conceal me in a triangle of shame. I ran my thumb down the wallpaper in the corner till it split.

Dad came home from work and I heard him say, "Where's Doris? Where is my girl?"

Mum sent Bobby to get something from the outhouse and then told dad that I was in disgrace. There was a muffled conversation, and, in an agony of embarrassment, she told my father of the shocking thing I had said.

"I have punished her to make sure she never uses that word again," she said.

I have never felt the least desire to.

CHAPTER
TWENTY

Dad and Uncle Arnold decided to join the village cricket team.

"Just the thing, a cricket match on a Saturday afternoon," they said. So, resplendent in their white flannels and with their families accompanying them, they arrived on the village sports field every Saturday afternoon. Our mothers wore their best straw hats, with gossamer-fine veil tied over their faces and hair. Mum had little butterflies on hers and Auntie Madge had one with flowers on. They both looked beautiful and remote.

Mollie and I wore our best shantung silk dresses and Panama hats. We both thought we looked very nice. The boys wore their best suits, too. It was quite a splendid day for us all.

All the ladies sat together and chatted about this and that and clapped their hands delicately when the players scored a run. We children were allowed to go and play as the game progressed, because they thought children couldn't be expected to sit still for long.

At half time, we were given tea. This was made in an urn in the pavilion. It was ghastly. I drank it with a shudder for every sip, but I so enjoyed the large slice of shop-made Dundee cake that went with it that I suffered the tea in case a complaint deprived me of the cake. It was considered that shop cake was very inferior to home-made, which is probably why I enjoyed it so much.

One afternoon, when we were playing, we saw some boys from the village come into our field. We started strutting about and talking rather loudly to make sure they noticed us. Then they came over to us.

"Wanna play?" they said. Did we want to play? Wild horses wouldn't stop us. They taught us leapfrog, piggy-in-the-middle and lots of new words. We did enjoy ourselves.

The match was over, and I saw Dad walking from the pitch with his team. I ran towards him, and, wishing to impress him with my newly acquired knowledge, I flung my arms round his legs, looked into his face and said sweetly, "Hello, bloody fool." There was an audible gasp and then dead silence, followed by a stinging slap on my bottom. My Daddy had hit me; my dear kind Daddy had hit me! I was almost dancing with the pain. His bright eyes were hurt, appealing to his friends to understand that his little daughter didn't know what she was saying.

"Never speak to me like that again," he said. "That is a word ladies never use."

Somehow I didn't enjoy cricket matches very much after that. I preferred it when we played at home.

Wishing to get as much practice as possible, Dad and Uncle Arnold made their own cricket pitch in the field outside our garden. They rolled and mowed until they had made a fair sized level patch, adequate for bowling practice. Uncle Arnold was considered a demon bowler, and he was also a good batsman. What Dad lacked in skill he made up for in enthusiasm.

Most summer evenings, we played cricket, and this continued all my childhood days. By the time I was fourteen, I could bowl as well as any boy and hold my own with a bat.

CHAPTER
TWENTY-ONE

Granddad started taking long walks around the countryside. He could often be seen chatting to the workers in the fields, and he made many friends. He liked a glass of stout and would call at the off-licence across the fields. The off-licence was also the general store, and I was often sent to buy matches or sugar for my mother. There were long wooden seats inside with little tables and more outside, where men sat to drink their beer on hot summer days. Well-trodden paths in every direction led to this little establishment.

Granddad used to sit there with the other men, "putting the world to rights" as my mother called it. They called him "squire". He was invited to their cottages and his advice sought about "a bit of bother" they were having.

It was amazing how they congregated at the off-licence when they saw him crossing the field. I didn't realise then that this was most likely due to his greeting of, "What are you having boys?"

"He always was a soft touch," my mother would remark.

Even so, I am sure their respect for each other was mutual.

* * *

This was the year of the drought. Granddad came in one day and said the men couldn't see any signs of a break in the weather.

"Things are getting pretty bad," he said.

Scorching sun had dried the grass and cracked the ground in the dusty fields. The water in our wells was getting low. We couldn't bath; a bowl of water was all that could be spared for personal hygiene. Despite this, we managed to wash all over and then the water was saved to wash small items of clothing. Then it was put in the jugs in the closet, disinfectant added and poured down the lavatory. At all costs the closet must be kept in a sanitary condition.

One morning, Bobby and I were playing in the field. I was picking a few poppies. They seemed among the few wild flowers surviving. The dogs were with us as usual. For no apparent reason, Rover started to bark very loudly, and we laughed at him because he usually only barked at strangers or in play. He became very agitated and kept nudging us towards the house. My mother heard his bark and knew better than to ignore it. She came across the field and found that we were close to a nest of adders. She picked up a lump of earth and threw it, and they slithered down a crack in the ground.

Instinct must have warned Rover of the danger, for as far as we knew, he had never seen a snake before.

The next evening, I was helping to collect the eggs, when I put my hand in the nest box and felt something flap against it. I peered inside and saw to my horror another snake with a half-swallowed frog in its mouth.

It had taken the frog headfirst, and its back legs were sticking out each side of its mouth. It was a sickening sight. I know that the frog saved me from being bitten. It probably also saved my life because the snake was another adder. To this day, a snake has the ability to chill my spine.

It seemed it would never rain. We were unable to enjoy the lovely weather because of the fear of being without water. We were thirsty, but could only have a small quantity of water to drink. Some people suffered more than we did. Inevitably, children came to school in unwashed clothes, and personal cleanliness was difficult to maintain.

A man called at our house with a horse-drawn water wagon. He sold us water for three farthings a bucket. My mother bought as many as she could afford and had them poured into the well. She was worried that she was asking for too much, in case it deprived someone else.

The head mistress was discussing the drought with my mother after school one day, and I heard her say "Nits", and then she advised my mother to have my hair cut short. My mother, not wishing us to join the afflicted, took us to the village barber to have our hair cut. Bobby also had a mop of curls. Mum explained we'd be cooler in the hot weather, and this explanation satisfied us. It was lovely not to have curlers put in my hair at night. My mother had always wound the bottom twelve inches in rags so that the ringlets would stay tidy during the day. Quite a lot of children appeared at school with their heads devoid of hair, but I just accepted that it was to make them more comfortable in the heat.

I spent a lot of time sitting in the fir tree in the front garden. There was a comfortable branch not too far up, and there I sat with a book, too listless to do anything else.

Just after I arrived home from school one day, we noticed that the wild birds were silent; the air had become sultry and the heat oppressive. Not a leaf stirred. Dad was home earlier than usual, and as he came in, he said, "I think we are going to have a storm. We had better get the ducks and chickens into their sheds and make sure all the animals are in, too."

I found Smut, then we called the dogs, who came running. Then we all went to help with the ducks and chickens. Katy's kids had been Billies, so they had been given away. Many years later, I learned that they had provided two needy families with meat.

The sky was now almost black, and a few large drops of rain fell, making dark rings of moisture on the parched ground.

"Into the house quickly," called my mother, and we all ran as fast as we could. In a howling fury, the wind sprang upon the trees, hurling them from side to side. It grew dark as night, and then there was a blinding flash, which looked as if it stabbed the ground, and another tore across the sky. A crash of thunder split the air just as it reached the house. I was terrified and so was Bobby.

"There's nothing to be afraid of," Dad said. "It's only the clouds bumping together. When they bump, they burst, and then the rain comes down."

I have already said our father could make up good stories. Anyway, after that explanation, storms never worried us, and by the time we knew what really happened, we had survived enough not to worry anyway.

"It's a good thing I managed to catch the earlier train tonight," Dad said. "I would have been on my way from the station in this otherwise."

The rain fell in torrents, flattening the plants in the garden, filling the ditches and eventually our wells and the duck pond.

After the storm was over, we put on our boots and went for a walk in the sweet fresh air. The countryside smelled clean, the half-withered flowers were standing up again and the wild birds were bathing in the puddles.

We let the chickens out into their runs where they had a feast of worms, and the ducks made straight for the pond. It was not yet very deep, but it made no difference to their enjoyment.

We took Rover and Jackie with us, and when we came to the Dragonfly pond, Rover plunged in and splashed in the water, with his tongue lolling out and his eyes rolling in ecstasy. We tried to persuade Jackie to join him, but he just retreated a little further from the pond and sat down. He didn't mind getting his feet wet in the grass, but that was as far as he would go. He

70

looked extremely puzzled by Rover's behaviour, and Daddy said, "Who's afraid of the water, then?"

Jackie looked sheepish, and his eyes shifted from side to side.

"You are a coward Jackie," Mum said, laughing.

This would never do. My dog a coward? My dog afraid of water? I devised a plan. The next afternoon, I found a long piece of rope and tied it to Jackie's collar.

"Come, Jack. We're going for a walk," I said.

He trotted along behind me, and Bobby followed with Rover. We came to the duck pond, and at the side I told Jackie to sit. Still clutching the rope, I walked round the pond until I was on one side and Jackie on the other.

"Now Jack, jump," I said and gave the rope a tug, thinking he would have to leap in the water. He did jump, but backwards. One minute I was on the bank and the next in mid-air over the pond, still hanging onto the rope. I seemed to hover in the air for a moment, and then I was in the water up to my waist. Something had gone terribly wrong.

Bobby was crying and saying, "You naughty girl. I'll tell Mummy if you don't get out."

As if I could conceal the fact anyway!

Rover started barking, which brought my mother running down the garden. She grabbed a long piece of wood and held it out to me, and, clinging to it, I managed to wade out of the water. This wasn't very easy, because I had wellies on, and they were full of water, and the bottom of the pond was very muddy.

My mother hauled me up the bank, and I was a sorry sight, clad in green slime and smelling vilely of duck pond. I think it was the smell that reduced me to tears.

Fortunately the kettles of water were on the hob as usual, so a tin bath was brought into the kitchen and filled with hot water. I was made to wait outside the back door until everything was ready for my bath. My mother peeled off my offensive garments and flung them to the other side of the yard, saying, "Pooh!" and shuddering each time she removed one. She put them in a tub to soak. Soaking in the hot bath, I said tearfully, "I was only trying to teach Jackie to swim."

"If it hadn't been for the drought, that water would have been over your head, my girl," my mother replied. "Don't you ever do such a stupid thing again."

CHAPTER
TWENTY-TWO

During the rest of the summer, we had our usual influx of visitors. We had trips to the seaside, picnics by the river and games in the field. We helped with haymaking and went gleaning in the cornfields. Our relations from London thought it was wonderful.

It must have been very hard work for my mother — entertaining so many people. Some were very considerate and helped with the housework and cooking, so Mum was free to share the fun, but others came with the idea of having a holiday, and a holiday they had! Although it was never mentioned in my presence, I could always tell which ones my mother was most pleased to see. I too had my favourites.

The house seemed very quiet when they had all left.

One Uncle and Aunt arrived with their very pampered daughter, and the very next day Kaiser disgraced us by getting out and chasing her into the barn, where she started bawling. She was so unnerved by the experience, that she refused to leave the house without her parents, and they left a couple of days later, never to come again. The rooster never even got near her, because we saw him coming and told her to run into the barn with us.

My mother's other brother, my Uncle Tom, also came to stay and said he wasn't going to be intimidated by a silly old cockerel. Kaiser was in the run with the hens at the time, and Uncle Tom said he'd go and collect the eggs. As soon as he entered the run, the rooster leapt on his back, and he beat a hasty retreat. We had all gathered to watch the fun, knowing exactly what would happen. Uncle Tom laughed as much as we did and said he'd never have believed it.

Our school holiday was now over, and we returned to school on a misty September morning. It was always rather exciting when we opened our new exercise books. The smell of new pencils, little boys playing 'conkers' and little girls bringing their skipping-ropes to school, meant the Autumn term.

September drifted into October, and we started to gather in the crops for the winter. Then dead Michaelmas Daises, Golden Rod and all the other faded plants were cut down and piled into a heap in the field. Everything that would burn was collected and thrown onto the heap, for this would be our Guy Fawkes Night bonfire. Daddy and Uncle Arnold bought us fireworks, and Mollie and Dennis helped Bobby and me to make a Guy. Any local children who wished to join us on the night were welcome. Potatoes were put in the ashes under the kitchen range, and by the time the firework display was over, they were cooked. All the children had one with butter, pepper and salt. They were delicious, and the cup of hot cocoa that went with it never tasted better.

Our bonfire night was an excellent way of getting rid of the rubbish and garden refuse, and the children who joined in looked on it as a great event.

Each season brought it's own special treat. There was always something to look forward to.

CHAPTER
TWENTY-THREE

By this time we had become very self-sufficient. Our vegetable plot produced enough potatoes, carrots, turnips, onions, swedes and parsnips to see us through the winter. We always had a plentiful supply of winter cabbage and Brussel Sprouts. Greengage and plums were bottled. Shallots were pickled and surplus tomatoes were made into chutney. We also had a good store of Strawberry, Raspberry, Blackcurrant and Blackberry and Apple jams. Eggs were "put down" in crocks containing a preserving solution and lasted until the hens started laying again. All the young cockerels were fattened and made a very acceptable gift at Christmas for our many relations and friends. My father became adept at killing them quickly and painlessly and my mother prepared them for the table; even I helped with the plucking. In retrospect, I wonder how I did it. One thing I do know is that Mum could never eat poultry. Now I understand why.

On the first of December, Bobby and I started the ritual of crossing off the days to Christmas. Each evening the calendar was put on the table, and we crossed off the day. Dad always made us understand that the good things in life had to be earned, so each evening if we had been good and helpful we were given a good mark and this was written by our names on the calendar. If we had been naughty or disobedient, a mark was deducted. We had to earn enough marks to make us worthy of the presents Father Christmas would bring. It was strange on Christmas Eve — our totals were exactly the same.

The night Dad came home from work and said, "I'm not going to work for three days", we knew we hadn't long to wait. We made paper-chains and went out and collected evergreens. The parlour was decorated with tinsel and brightly coloured balls. By the time our paper-chains were hung and the holly and ivy draped around the pictures, it looked very festive.

On Christmas Eve, Bobby and I would kneel solemnly by the fireplace in the parlour and call up the chimney to Father Christmas for a longed-for doll or toy, and we were allowed to add, "And anything else you can spare." Our bedtime story that night would be the *Christmas Story*, and afterwards we sang, *Away in a Manger*. Then up to bed, where we hung one of Mum's black woollen stockings on our bed post.

Oh, the thrill of waking on Christmas morning, dressing quickly and running with our stockings to the kitchen fireside to explore them. I was in my seventh heaven until I pulled out a very realistic, jointed, wooden snake. I screamed and flung it from me. Mum tried to console me, and Dad showed me it was made of wood. But my recent confrontation with the snake in the nest had made it totally unacceptable. It was thrown outside in the yard before I would allow Dad to empty the rest of the stocking for me.

After breakfast, we went into the parlour and opened some more presents, which were waiting by the fireplace. What a magical morning it was. Our every wish seemed to be granted. We spent the morning playing with our new toys, and in the afternoon we played games or listened to the gramophone. After tea, Dad read aloud to us from our new storybooks. We grew drowsy sitting in the glow of the fire, and the oil lamp illuminated our little circle, sending long shadows into the corners of the room. Tucked in to bed that night, feeling wonderfully warm and loved, we fell asleep in a state of complete happiness.

CHAPTER
TWENTY-FOUR

Every spring, the house was cleaned thoroughly from top to bottom. All the paintwork was washed and polished, including that on the balcony. Curtains and quilts, loose covers on the furniture and cushion covers were washed. All the windows were flung open to get rid of the winter fug, and the house smelt of disinfectant, wax polish and fresh air.

There was a lady who lived alone with her son in a mean little cottage not far away. She was desperately poor and took any work that was available to earn a livelihood. Sometimes she worked in the fields and at others, cleaning for anybody who could offer her a few hours employment. I think it must have been her plight that prompted Mum to ask her to come and help with the spring-cleaning. She was happy to come for a good mid-day meal and a few shillings, which was all my mother could afford. She brought her son, Wilfrid, with her, as it was during the school Easter holiday that the spring-cleaning was done.

Whilst Mrs Bond was working, we were expected to play with Wilfrid. He was about nine years old. Poor Wilfrid hadn't one attractive feature. His round glasses sat on the end of his raw, moist nose, and his vacant red-rimmed eyes peered through thick lenses. His large top teeth hung over his bottom lip, and even his hands had a horny appearance. He was furtive, sly and quite repulsive in his habits. No matter how I tried, I couldn't like him.

One day I was holding Smut, who was lying on his back purring happily while I tickled him under the chin, when Wilfrid said, "I dare touch the cat's bottom and lick my fingers," and so saying, he did exactly that. Bobby and I drew back with horrified gasps, and Smut, who was very affronted by such treatment, struggled free from my arms and dashed away.

I was very glad when the spring-cleaning was finished, and we could look forward to our preparations for our annual visitors.

The evenings were light now, and when Dad came home from work, he would set about repairing the chicken houses and sowing seeds for summer flowers and autumn crops. Everything was fresh and new. The first signs of blossom were appearing on the fruit trees, and the garden was bright with spring flowers.

At the end of May, the letters started to arrive from our relatives, asking if it would be convenient to come for a few days in the summer, and when.

It was quite difficult to fit them all in.

One morning Dad opened a letter and said, "Grannie is coming to stay and is bringing your cousins, Malcolm and Mavis, with her."

I had never met my cousins, and had seen Grannie only once when I was very small. I had heard Dad and

Auntie Beatie talking about her and laughing about an incident in their childhood:

Auntie Beatie said, "Do you remember how we had to line up each Friday night for the cane?" and they both laughed and started telling Mum how Grannie believed in discipline. She had had nine children, two had died in infancy, but she had brought up the rest on "discipline" and the belief that "children should be seen and not heard". My paternal Grandfather was just a background figure, seldom seen, as he spent most of the time at home in his "den" with his books.

Apparently, the lining up for the cane was to show the children what they'd get if they were naughty. One story went: each Friday they had to wait outside the parlour door and take their turn to go in — eldest first, youngest last. When Grannie was comfortably seated, each child was called in: Auntie Mabel was first, then Auntie Beatie, then Dad. When it was Auntie Beatie's turn, Dad gave her a playful shove, which sent her hurtling into the room.

"You'll get an extra stroke for that my girl," sad Grannie sternly.

"But Bertie pushed me," pleaded Auntie Beatie.

"And another for telling tales," was the reply.

There were many little anecdotes like that, and by the time Grannie arrived, I was quite apprehensive.

My first glimpse of her convinced me that I must be very good indeed. Her unyielding, corseted figure was clad from head to foot in shining black satin, and her straw hat was secured on her head with two stout hatpins.

I made my first mistake within a couple of hours of her arrival. My mother was playing with me, and began to tickle me. I was thoroughly enjoying the fun, but I gasped through my laughter, "Don't Mummy, don't."

Grannie, in a stentorian voice said, "'Don't Mummy' indeed. She is your mother. She has the right to do what she likes with you."

Mum's face was inscrutable, but she gave me a little smile so I knew she wasn't cross with me, even if Grannie was. Somehow, though, the game wasn't any fun after that.

"What all children need is a good dose of Castor Oil once a week," Grannie said to my mother one morning.

"I don't believe in dosing children," my mother replied.

That evening, when Mum was out feeding the chickens, Grannie made me line up with Malcolm and Mavis. Out came the Castor Oil. Malcolm and Mavis took theirs quietly, and then it was my turn. It looked and smelt revolting. I decided I wouldn't take it and firmly closed my mouth. Grannie pinched my nose, so that I couldn't breathe, forcing me to open my mouth. In went the Castor Oil. She held my jaw firmly until I had swallowed it. Then she released her hold on me. I was in tears and spluttering against the horrid stuff. Through my coughing, I heard Mum come in, then there were a few muttered words from my mother to Grannie. Mum said, "Go out and play children," and we all trouped outside. Bobby didn't have to take his dose.

I spent a miserable morning the following day, trotting backwards and forwards to the closet. I felt very pleased when I overheard Mum telling Grannie never to give her children medicine again without consulting her first.

During the afternoon, my Auntie Hilda and her husband arrived. They were the parents of Malcolm and Mavis. Uncle Douglas was an Army Officer, who had spent a lot of time in Africa. He had recently returned, bringing with him an African Grey parrot, named George. He was going abroad again and wanted a home for George.

"We'll have him," said Mum. "What is one more among so many?" So that day George entered our lives. He was great fun and talked a lot, but he spoilt all our games of hide-and-seek, because he soon learned to call, "Coo-ee" exactly as we did when we were ready to be found. This brought the seeker searching before the hider had hidden, and the game had to be abandoned.

Grannie was going to look after Malcolm and Mavis whilst their parents were abroad. They all left the next day, and I felt very sorry for my cousins, as I knew it was their fate to have a dose of Castor Oil every week for a year.

A few days later, Dad was working in the garden, and I was helping him to pull out the weeds. I saw Mr Wise, who lived in a rather tumble-down building across the field near the off-licence, come striding towards us, looking very red in the face and extremely angry.

"I want a word with you," he said to Dad in a very belligerent manner.

"Certainly," said Dad in his usual friendly way.

"What do you mean by whistling at my missus every time she passes your house," he said, poking Dad in the chest with a bony finger.

"Really old chap, I don't know what you are talking about," Dad replied, looking puzzled.

"Make her out to be a liar, would you?" said Mr Wise, drawing his hand into a fist.

"No, I really don't understand." Then the light dawned on his face. "Perhaps it was the parrot. We've only had him a few days. Perhaps that's what it was."

"Garn, tell me another."

"Come and see," said Dad. They went into the house, and Mum was surprised to see our visitor. He wasn't a very sociable man. "Mr Wise would like to see the parrot," Dad said by way of explanation, giving my mother a wink to warn her to be careful what she said.

Dad tried to persuade George to whistle, but he refused to co-operate. He just stared at Mr Wise, turning his head almost upside down to get a better view.

"Come into the hall where he can't see you. He's a bit shy with strangers," Dad said. Still George remained silent. It was quite obvious Mr Wise wasn't convinced. He went out muttering, "If it happens again, you'll have me to answer to." Just as he said that, George gave the sauciest whistle imaginable. "Alright I heard," said Mr Wise.

As soon as they could decently close the door, my parents gave way to uncontrollable laughter. I laughed, too, because they were laughing, although I didn't really understand why.

"Gosh, he must think I'm hard up," chortled Dad. "With a face like that, she'd be safe anywhere."

Actually, I thought Mrs Wise had a face like a withered potato.

CHAPTER
TWENTY-FIVE

My father took his annual leave in July. His brother Philip and his wife, Rose, came to stay for a fortnight, bringing with them their sons, Douglas and Graham. I loved my uncle and aunt, they were so jolly, and everyone laughed a lot in their company. Douglas was my senior by six months and very protective towards me, which I thoroughly enjoyed. We were really good friends, and Bobby and Graham got on well together, too.

We had a wonderful holiday. Some days we travelled to Southend and from there took sea trips to other resorts along the coast. We played on the beach and paddled in the sea. Even our parents put on bathing costumes and dabbled in the shallows with us. They could all swim, too, and when we said we would like to learn, they brought us "water wings". They were made of some sort of cotton fabric, and we had to wet them thoroughly and blow them up. The air gradually escaped, making little bubbles on the surface of the material, so they didn't stay inflated for long. Consequently, they didn't give us much confidence.

Our parents thought they were very modern in their bathing costumes. They were made of very thin, stretchy stockinette and with a high neckline and little sleeves and legs that reached almost to the knee, they were very modest garments indeed — when they were dry. When they stepped out of the water — oh, dear! The neckline stretched almost to the waist, and the entire garment had descended woefully and clung to the body like a drooping skin, so that every nook and cranny was revealed in its entirety. I didn't know where to look and ground my toe into the sand and pretended to be looking very hard at something out at sea.

Mum and Auntie Rose were sitting on the beach after their swim. They decided it was time for our picnic lunch, and they were chatting together as they prepared it. I heard the words, "Castor Oil" and pricked up my ears in dread, but realised my mother was only telling Auntie Rose about Grannie dosing me with it.

"Yes, I had a bull and a cow with her over that," Auntie Rose said.

"Really, the things grown up say," I said to myself. "If I had said that, I bet it would be called a naughty word."

We were all very sorry when the time came for them to return to London, and we waved them off, knowing they would surely spend a holiday with us again as soon as possible.

CHAPTER
TWENTY-SIX

A coupe of weeks later, Auntie Mabel and Uncle Arthur came to spend their holiday with us. They had two daughters, Phyllis and Muriel. Auntie Mabel was my father's eldest sister.

My first sight of Phyllis astounded me. I had never seen anyone so thin. She was muffled up in a thick coat, scarf and hat even though it was a warm summer's day. Her poor little face was pinched and white, and her legs were like sticks. She had suffered from Rickets Disease, an all too common affliction amongst children born at the end of the 1914-1918 war, owing to the deficiency of essential foods. Just as she was recovering from this, she was stricken with Rheumatic Fever, a long and debilitating illness. She was so frail that I thought she would disintegrate when her coat and hat were taken off. My mother suggested I take her to see the ducks and chickens and to play in the garden for a while until dinner was ready. The fresh air would give her an appetite. But she was apathetic and difficult to play with.

After a week, her parents were ready to return to London, and my mother suggested they leave Phyllis with us for the rest of the summer, so that she could recover from her illness. Fresh eggs and milk were readily available, and we had fresh vegetables and fruit from the garden.

"You won't know her in a week or two," said my mother persuasively. She said it would be a good idea to let her play without a hat and coat, so that the sun could get to her body, as this would strengthen her. Mum promised to do it very gradually, so that she wouldn't get a chill. "I'll look after her as though she were my own," she added.

I wasn't very keen on the idea of her staying. I just couldn't understand a child who didn't want to run in the fields or romp in the hay. I thought her "soppy". She was about four years older than me but seemed much younger. When my mother explained to me that she had been ill so long, she had forgotten how to play and that I must teach her, so that she could be happy again, I took her under my wing and mothered her, and before long, we got on well together.

After a few weeks, her skinny frame filled out, and the colour gradually returned to her face. Her limbs became tanned and her lank hair springy and glossy. Soon, she was running and exploring the hedgerows with me, and I took pleasure in teaching her how to make daisy chains. We found a blackbird's nest with little blue eggs in it, and we'd peep in each day to see if the chicks had hatched. This was a new experience for her, and I told her we must look without touching in case the birds deserted the nest. Her delight when the young ones arrived gave a tremendous pleasure. Her enthusiasm for games returned, and we played hide and seek in the orchard. She had never known such freedom. She even felt bold enough to say, "I'm going to make friends with that silly old rooster." As she approached his run, he flung himself against the wire, and she retreated hastily. We collapsed with laughter. He looked such an idiot leaping about with his feathers spread in futile assault.

When Phyllis' parents came to fetch her in September, they could hardly believe their eyes. Her legs were sturdy, and her skin glowed. She looked a picture of health. She didn't want to go back to London, but when my mother told her she could come again next summer, she went off quite happily.

To this day, Phyllis says, "You know, Pengelly was the making of me."

CHAPTER
TWENTY-SEVEN

Later in the year, about November I think, Mum and I were doing the washing up after tea, when we heard a tremendous crash upstairs in Granddad's room, which was directly above the kitchen. It made me jump so much, that I dropped the cup I was holding.

Mum ran upstairs, and then we heard a window flung open, followed by another crash in the yard outside, then a dragging sound across the floor above. Bobby and I stared at each other wide-eyed, wondering what was happening.

When Mum came down, I noticed that her face had gone all white, and her hands were shaking. Putting on her coat, she told Bobby and me to sit on the chesterfield, and we were not to move until she came back. She said Granddad had had a fall, and she was going down to Mrs West's house to telephone the doctor. Mrs West lived on the road just where it joined the cart track.

We sat on the chesterfield for what seemed a very long time, so overcome by the seriousness of the situation we didn't even speak.

Mum returned with a man we didn't recognise at first, because we had only seen him in the daytime working on his farm.

"Mr Patmore has come to help me lift Granddad into bed," she said.

I remember thinking how nice he looked in his suit. After a while they came down and Mr Patmore said, "Goodnight little uns; be good," and to my mother, "Let us know if you need any help my girl."

Something very bad had happened. Mummy never needed help. She always helped other people. She always lent a helping hand if anyone was ill or in trouble.

I was very relieved when Dad came home from work. He hadn't been in for more than ten minutes when the doctor arrived. He went upstairs with Mummy. Dad said we must be very quiet because Granddad was very ill.

After a while the doctor came downstairs with Mum and said, "I'm afraid the old gentleman has had a stroke."

I didn't know what had actually happened until I was much older. When he fell, Granddad had knocked over the oil lamp, and my mother had entered the room to find the tablecloth and curtains blazing. She had flung open the window, scooped up the lamp in the tablecloth and thrown it out of the window. Then she tore down the curtains, and they followed. She grabbed a cushion and beat out the remaining flames with it. She said it was terrifying, because she knew she shouldn't have opened the window, but there was no alternative. Granddad had fallen across the hearth and she dragged him to a place of safety in the middle of the floor. Pausing only long enough to be sure the fire was out, she had grabbed her coat and stumbled across the pitch-black fields to summon help. Mum was only a small woman as I have already mentioned, but she had dealt with the situation in her usual calm manner, avoiding what could have been a terrible disaster.

Granddad was very feeble after his illness. He partly regained his power of speech, but one arm and leg remained very weak. He needed constant care, and it was impossible to leave the house for long unless someone was available to stay with him. His many friends called constantly to see how the "Squire" was getting on, and it was touching to see how concerned they were. Their visits meant a lot to him.

CHAPTER
TWENTY-EIGHT

The following August, Granddad suffered another stroke, and this time it left him almost totally incapacitated. My mother had to wash, dress and feed him, and his speech was unintelligible. Bobby and I no longer went to his room, as he no longer understood that we were his grandchildren. It distressed us and agitated him.

When I returned to school in September, my mother was unable to take me even part of the way, because she could not leave Granddad for more than a few minutes. He could still manage to shuffle around very slowly, but his intellect was impaired, and she was afraid he would come to harm.

She asked Jessie, who lived in a cottage nearby, if she would take me and bring me back in the afternoon. I was only eight years old and had about two and a half miles to walk to school through country lanes.

"I will give you a sixpence a week for your trouble," Mum told her. Jessie glanced at the sixpence, smiled and said, "Yes, I'll do it".

"Thank you," said Mum and handed over the money. Sixpence doesn't sound much these days, but then it would buy a pair of plimsolls, a saucepan or even a yard of dress material.

I said goodbye to my mother who hurried back to the house and started on my way to school with Jessie. She was about thirteen years old and a big buxom girl. I thought her almost a woman.

"Your Mother put me in charge of you," said Jessie as soon as Mum was out of sight. "So you must do as I tell you. The first thing you do is carry my satchel." The satchel was heavy, and I had my own to carry as well. It didn't occur to me to refuse, because I had seen Mum hand the money to Jessie and thought doing as I was told was part of the bargain.

Sometimes a farmer would give us a lift on his cart, and it was lovely to be relieved of the weight I carried. I would sit there, entranced, watching the horse's huge haunches rising and falling as he plodded his way along the road. Best of all, I liked to ride on the hay cart in summer. As we left school in the afternoon, the men were returning from the fields, and they would toss us up into the pile of hay and carry us home. We used to lie there in the scented softness, with the hay prickling our bare legs, almost lulled to sleep by the gentle motion as we passed from bright sunlight into the cool of leafy lanes.

One morning, when I was walking to school with Jessie, she said, "Hold out your hand, I have a surprise for you."

Eagerly I held out my hand, and the surprise was a hard slap. This was the first of many such episodes, and

I began to feel quite apprehensive about my walks to and from school.

On our way back one afternoon, we found some acorns. The boys pulled the seed from the cup and put the stalks in their mouths and pretended they were smoking pipes.

Jessie put some acorns in my hand and said, "Eat them."

"I'm not allowed to," I said, because I had been cautioned against eating seeds and berries of any kind in case they were poisonous.

The other children had walked on.

"Pigs eat them, so you can eat them, too," Jessie went on.

Still I protested.

"If you don't eat them, I'll bash your brains in. Anyway, we won't go home till you do." She took hold of my arm and twisted it behind my back. It hurt a great deal, and I was very frightened about not going home, so, in the end I ate them. They were horrible. I suppose I ate five or six and was in tears the whole time. "Wipe your eyes. Don't let your mother see you have been blubbing; she will think you are a baby," Jessie urged. She must have realised that traces of tears would have led to questions being asked.

As I approached Pengelly, Mum came across the field to meet me and told me a friend of Daddy's known to us as Uncle Alf had come to see us in his new motorcar. Uncle Alf was a very little man whose face was always wreathed in smiles. "A little man with a big heart" was the way people described him. He and Dad had been friends since school days. We liked him a lot.

"Let's go for a ride," he said. He helped Mum bring Granddad downstairs, and they got him settled in the car. This was a treat — a real motorcar. Granddad seemed to enjoy the ride. He looked about him with a puzzled but happy expression. We sped along the country lanes, and people stopped to watch us pass. I felt like a Queen.

Then I found I wasn't enjoying it so much. I felt funny. Bt the time we arrived home, I had pains in my tummy, and I felt very sick.

"Travel sickness," the grown-ups decided.

Later that night, I was very ill indeed. Violent pains developed, and my head ached unbearably. My insides were churning, and I vomited on and off all night. The next day, I lay on the chesterfield in the kitchen feeling dreadful. I was normally a very robust child. I don't remember ever having such an ordinary ailment as a cold and couldn't understand what was happening to me. This condition went on for several days. The sight of food nauseated me. I only had to see a glass of milk, and my stomach would start heaving. Even the blandest of foods were rejected, and I grew thin and weak.

Mummy asked me if I had eaten anything she didn't know about. I said, "No", then remembered the acorns. She must have noticed that something had registered in my mind, because she said, "Don't be afraid to tell me."

"I mustn't tell tales. You told me I mustn't," I replied.

"You are not telling tales when I ask you," Mum answered. And so the whole story came out. My mother was furious; she had been paying Jessie to bully me.

Jessie had a rather unfortunate home life, which is probably why my mother asked her to take me to school. I expect she felt she would like the money. I had never seen her mother or heard her mentioned. So maybe she had died or no longer lived there. I had noticed that her father was a strange man who never seemed to be able to walk in a straight line, but wandered all over the road. "Boosey by name and Boosey by nature", I heard it said, although I did not understand then what it meant.

This may have accounted for the brutal streak in Jessie. I don't think she had known much kindness.

Mr Patmore called one morning saying that he hadn't seen me pass the farm in the mornings and was wondering if everything was alright. He thought perhaps Granddad was worse, and he came to see if Mum needed any help.

When he saw me lying there on the chesterfield, he asked, "What's the matter, princess?" He always called me that.

Mum explained what had happened.

"Take her to Southend for the day, my girl," he said to Mum. "Let her sit on the beach and inhale the vapours at low tide. That'll put her right."

The local people had great faith in the therapeutic qualities of the air at Southend. When the tide went right out, a great expanse of mud was laid bare and the theory was that the sun drew into the air the healing qualities it contained.

"I can't leave my father alone," Mum replied.

"Don't worry about that. My missus will come and take care of the old gent and the little un," he said "Give her that day at the sea, and don't fret."

Still feeling very ill, I travelled to Rayleigh station on the back of Mum's bike, and we took the train to Southend.

I took no joy in the outing, but I sat on the beach all day and even managed a cheese sandwich without being sick. Mummy thought it was very encouraging and that, soon, I would be better.

I arrived home in a state of complete exhaustion, but from that day, my appetite returned, and soon I was back to normal good health. Whether I was recovering anyway and this was pure coincidence, or whether there was any truth in the local remedy, I will never know. There was certainly no doubt in the minds of our friends at the farm.

For the rest of the term, I was taken to school by a lad called Tommy. He was nearly fourteen and very kind to me. He carried my satchel and protected me from Jessie. He had to be persuaded to take the sixpence a week. Several times I heard him tell Jessie to, "stop picking on the smaller children".

One day, as we were coming home from school, we saw the baker's van coming along at a fair trot. Tommy told me to stand at the side of the road with him till it passed. Jessie was on the other side of the road. She called me to come and stand with her. Tommy put a restraining hand on my shoulder.

"Alright stay there and get killed," she shouted.

I panicked and ran across the road, just as the pony drew level. I saw flailing hooves above me as the animal reared up on its hind legs and the baker standing up in the van with the reins pulled tight. I didn't realise how close to death I had been, but the baker did and told my mother, completely exonerating Tommy.

She was very cross with me for being so stupid and asked why I did it. I told her that Jessie had said I would get killed if I stayed where I was and that I was frightened. Mum didn't say anymore but seemed to immediately understand.

She was at her wits' end. She had the worry of her father's failing health, a small son to look after and the anxiety of the things that were happening to me.

The school term ended within a few days, and it so happened that Auntie Madge had heard of a lady who had started a small private school. It was about halfway along the road between their house and ours.

They had decided to send Mollie there next term, as it would be nearer for her, and thought it might be the answer to our present problem.

Bobby would be five soon and ready to start school. Dad suggested Mum went along to see Mrs Moss and ask whether she could take us next term. So he stayed with Granddad, while Mum took us to see the lady on the next Saturday morning.

After a brief talk, it was all arranged. I wasn't at all impressed. The "schoolroom" was just a room in her house, and I thought Mrs Moss rather "swanky". Now I would describe her as condescending. She behaved as though she thought she was a great lady. School was morning only and would we please be punctual.

Mum took me to say goodbye to the Headmaster and Headmistress at Hullbridge School, and I felt very sad. I had been happy there but felt quite pleased that I wouldn't have so far to go to school on rainy winter mornings.

Dad said he would buy me a little bike if I would try very hard to learn to ride it in time for school next term. Well, I did learn to ride it in three days, but there was one problem: I couldn't master the art of alighting. One day I was cycling along quite happily when Kaiser, who had escaped from the run again, spotted me and came hurtling after me.

"Mummy," I yelled. "Kaiser is chasing me."

Mum was taking in the washing at the time, and she grabbed the clothes prop and diverted him. I suddenly realised I had jumped off my bike in the approved manner, so I was now ready to ride to school. The roads were devoid of traffic in those days, except for an occasional horse and cart. A driver of a motor car always tooted the horn at everything in its path, so I would be quite safe.

Mum would have to leave Granddad in bed, put Bobby on the carrier of her bike and take us to school. She managed to do this in twenty minutes, so she left the curtains drawn in Granddad's bedroom and took

101

his breakfast up to him when she returned. It was the only thing she could do.

We made our own way home. Now that I could ride a bike, I found walking irksome, and, in no time, I had learned to sit Bobby on the seat and ride standing on the pedals. Soon this was how we went to school, too.

Mrs Moss didn't approve. She thought it very unladylike.

CHAPTER
TWENTY-NINE

There were three other girls at the school when we first arrived and one boy. The boy, named Tony, approached Bobby and said, "You're a tich aren't you?" Bobby went very pink, because everyone turned to look at him, and he didn't really understand what a "tich" was.

One of the girls was Mrs Moss's daughter, and her name was Daphne. Mollie and I arrived with our knee length boots shining to perfection and were very embarrassed when Daphne gave a smirk and said, "Here come the boot kids." All the children sniggered, and we tried to pull our skirts down as far as possible to hide the offending footwear. Until that moment, I had rather liked my boots, but when I looked at Daphne's patent leather ankle-strap shoes, my feet felt as though they had assumed gigantic proportions.

We began lessons, and I found them very uninteresting, because the standard of education I had received at Hullbridge School was far in advance of the instruction I received there.

The strange thing was that during term time, I received top marks for everything, but during the end of term examinations, Mrs Moss always announced that Daphne came top. Our parents were informed of this at the concert given by the children for the parents entertainment when the term ended. I can remember Auntie Madge silently mouthing ". . . and Daphne came top," to my mother when Mrs Moss gave her little speech, so it was obvious they knew what was happening. My mother's lips started twitching as she caught Auntie Madge's eye, and when she arrived home, she said to Dad (who had stayed with Granddad), "And guess who came top? But Doris was second."

We spent a lot of time learning the correct way to say "a round sound" and "each day in May we play" and precious little else.

I could tell my father was anxious that I didn't forget all I had learned at my previous school. We used to play sums and spelling for an hour each evening, so all in all I didn't do too badly, and I helped Bobby to read in the way I had been taught. I would be teacher and write words on a slate for him to copy, and I taught him to draw.

Without realising it, we were both learning.

CHAPTER
THIRTY

March came in like a lion. A howling gale was blowing, and rain and hail were lashing the windows. The wind screamed around the house and in the chimney. Darkness set in early.

"Daddy's late," said Mum, glancing anxiously at the clock. "But I don't suppose he'll be much longer." She put his slippers in the hearth to warm. "What a night. He will be soaked." Another half hour passed, then Dad arrived. He was drenched to the skin, and his coat was all muddy and torn. The wind had blown him off his bicycle into a ditch, and he was scratched and bleeding. Thorns were sticking in his face and eyelids. It took mother a long time to remove them with a fine sewing needle and a pair of tweezers. It must have been very painful. I had to hold a torch close to his face so that she could see better.

Dad had had to carry his bike the rest of the way home, because the front wheel had become buckled when he fell. He had also lost his hat.

"I've just about had enough of that journey," I heard him tell Mum.

He used my mother's bicycle to get to the station the next day. The weather continued cold and blustery, and as the temperature dropped, the rain turned to sleet, then to snow.

Uncle Phil, Auntie Rose and the boys were coming for the weekend, and I was filled with excitement at the prospect. By the time they arrived on the Friday evening it was snowing steadily. The next morning, we awoke to a pure white world. The snow was deep and powdery. Everything was transformed. I had never seen anything so entrancingly beautiful. I found it difficult to walk and had to step high as the snow came almost to the top of my boots.

Dad and Uncle Phil made us a snowman as tall as themselves. Rover and Jackie went wild. They rolled in the snow and rushed around with their muzzles searching the drifts, till little cones built up on the end of their noses. Beads of ice clung to the hair on the backs of their legs, and their bright pink tongues lolled from the side of their mouths as if they were smiling in ecstasy.

We had a wonderful time, and the boys didn't want to go back to London, but they had no choice as they had to go to school on Monday, and Uncle Phil had to go to work.

A few days later, the sun burst through the clouds, dazzling us with its brilliance. The snow sparkled as though sprinkled with a million diamonds, and then it started to melt. As evening approached, the sun went down, leaving a dull red sky, which tinted the snow pink. The melting snow turned to ice. This happened everyday for about a week, and icicles a yard long hung from the chicken house. Our snowman melted a little each day until it was just a lump in the field. The cart track became waterlogged, and we were cut off from the road. Dad had to wear a pair of fisherman's waders to get along the cart track. When he reached Mrs West's house, he left them there and changed into a pair of ankle length boots and continued to the station on foot.

The sky was leaden. The fields looked grey. Trees dripped, and everything was cold, damp and depressing.

Our lease on Pengelly would be up in June, and I think that winter made it easier for my parents to decide not to renew it. The thought of another one like it was almost too much to bear.

CHAPTER
THIRTY-ONE

Dad started to make enquires among his business colleagues regarding the possibility of finding a house to let which would be suitable for us.

One evening in early May he came home looking very pleased, as he had heard that Council houses were available in Letchworth, the new Garden City in Hertfordshire. One of his friends who lived there had invited him to spend the weekend with him so that he could have a look around and see if he liked the area. Mum was all for the idea and said if he saw a house he liked to go ahead and make arrangements for the move.

When he returned he said he had found a nice little house with quite a large garden. There was a school nearby which had a very good reputation, and the shops and railway station were only about ten minutes' walk away. He had made arrangements to take on the tenancy subject to confirmation within three days.

"It sounds fine. Let's make the move," said Mum.

They thought it best that Bobby and I left Mrs Moss's school at the end of the term, when we broke up for the Whitsun holiday, and when Uncle Arnold and Auntie Madge were told they said, "Good. Now that there can be no repercussions, Mollie can leave, too. We are going to send her back to her old school before she forgets everything she learned there."

When Mrs Moss was told, she said, "What a pity — just as they were getting on so nicely." She smiled at us, but I remember thinking that she looked as though she had a nasty taste in her mouth.

I certainly had no regrets about leaving.

The days ahead were filled with activity. Getting ready to move was a new game for Bobby and me.

One day when I was bustling around carrying out small errands for my mother, it suddenly registered on my mind that moving meant leaving Pengelly. How could we leave it? Never had it looked lovelier. The garden was brilliant with roses, and the scent surrounded us like an embrace. I walked around looking at everything as though seeing it for the first time. I sat on the swing dreamily pushing the ground with my toe from time to time to keep it in motion. Soon I would be living in some unknown place. I took deep breaths to lock the perfume of the roses inside me forever. I couldn't imagine life outside my little world. This is what sad means, I thought as a tear trickled down my cheek.

I think my parents noticed my despondency, because they were constantly telling me how nice our new home would be.

But there was another blow to fall. We would be allowed to keep one dog only at our house at Letchworth, and my Uncle Will had offered Jackie a home. Dad tried to soften the blow by telling me I'd see him again as he was going to live with my Uncle

Will. I cried and hugged Jackie and sobbed that I didn't want him to go.

"You know Uncle Will loves him. He will look after him," Dad said trying to console me. I hardly knew Uncle Will as he only paid us very brief visits and he seemed far away and unreal.

I never saw my little dog again. He ran out of Uncle Will's garden and was hit by a passing motorcar within days of leaving us. I wasn't told of this immediately, because I think Dad just didn't know where to begin. He waited until I had adjusted to being without him and then told me gently what had happened. I quite surprised myself by the calm way I took the news, but I had a little weep under the bedclothes that night.

"Katy won't be able to come with us because she needs a field to roam in, so she is going to live on the farm," said Mum casually one morning. "She will like it there because there are other goats to keep her company."

I suddenly found I didn't want to live in Letchworth. Everything would be different. The chickens and ducks were also going to the farm but this didn't trouble me too much. I did mind about leaving Katy, though. We put her on a chain and took her to her new home.

"Come on old girl," said Mr Patmore, and he took her to a paddock and released her. She trotted over to join the other goats without a backward glance. Seeing her go like that made it easier.

"Oh, Mr Patmore, I've been meaning to ask you. Do you want Kaiser or not? You know he is a bit of a handful, and I wouldn't want you to take him unless you are happy about it," said Mum.

110

"Yes, I have heard stories about him," he replied, his eyes twinkling. "I, too, have a rooster who rules the roost. Kaiser is too good a stock bird to be put down, so I'll take him, and they can sort it out between themselves."

It transpired that when Kaiser arrived on the farm, the resident cockerel was so incensed by the threat to his territory that he chased the newcomer all around the yard until Kaiser fled to a barn and took refuge under a pile of straw. We found ourselves saying "Poor old Kaiser" and wondering why we felt sorry for him. After all, he had chased each one of us at some time. Incredibly we found we had grown quite fond of him.

"It won't be very nice in our new home," I said, gloomily. "Not like Pengelly."

"Oh, it will," replied Mum. "You'll love it when you get used to it. The house is in a road. No more walking over muddy fields to get to school. And the lavatory will be in the house, and you'll only have to pull a chain, and water will pour down and wash the pan. We'll have a boiler behind the fire in the living room, and when we want a bath, there will be plenty of hot water. There is a lever over the sink in the kitchen, and you only have to switch it to the right, and hot water goes straight up the pipe to the bathroom. And what's more, we only have to turn a tap and the water comes out. No more pumping. We'll have gas lighting and a gas stove too."

"Yes and I have told you that your new school has lots of exciting activities like sports day and swimming lessons at the local swimming baths and singing festivals and lots of other interesting things," added Dad.

Maybe I would like it after all.

★ ★ ★

Soon, we had everything packed and brought down into the hall. Every piece of furniture that was light enough to carry had been brought downstairs. Wardrobes and chests of drawers would have to wait until the removal men arrived. The house began to look very empty, and the walls blank and unfriendly when the pictures were taken down. Only a dark square remained on the wallpaper to show where they had been. The fire in the kitchen range was allowed to go out so that Mum could clean out the ashes and give it a good polish before we left.

"We'll manage on the primus stove for cooking breakfast in the morning," she said the day before we left.

Uncle Arnold came to say goodbye to Granddad and stayed with him for awhile so that we could go and say goodbye to our friends.

That evening, we went for a last walk across the fields. Flocks of swallows were silhouetted against the sunset, and the song of the nightingale floated on the still air. We sat on a fallen tree trunk by the pond, and I noticed that the reflections in the water were so clear it looked as though trees were growing upside down. We stayed there quietly, our hearts too full to speak. The scent of the countryside enfolded us, and we were at peace.

"This is a memory to take with you. It will be special all your life," said Dad.

"I'll never forget Pengelly Daddy," I said. "Never."

CHAPTER
THIRTY-TWO

The next morning, we were up and dressed and had had breakfast by seven o'clock. Bobby and I stood by the front gate, watching for the removal van to arrive.

It was a perfect June day — June 20th, 1928 to be exact. The date has remained indelibly printed in my mind. Sparkling summer haze lay across the meadow. The earth was rock hard, and the driver was able to bring the van right up to the house.

My mother gave the men a cup of tea, and then work began in earnest. Bobby and I carried out a few small items and felt very much part of the operation. It was while I was fetching some oddments from the outhouse that I noticed the pear tree. It had bloomed late that year, and some blossom remained, but most of the petals were lying like a circular carpet on the ground below. I went to it and encircled its trunk with my arms, gazing up at the branches and noticed the minute pears, which were beginning to form. I wouldn't be there to eat the fruit ever again. I leaned my face against the trunk, and then I was diverted by my mother's call.

"Goodbye tree," I whispered.

I went into the kitchen, and Mum said, "I have put Smut in his travelling basket, so that he can't escape. We couldn't go without him, could we?" The lid of the basket had been securely fastened, and he was mewing plaintively.

Mum wrapped an old blanket around George's cage and tied it with string, and judging by the way he was attacking it, I thought there would be very little blanket left by the time we reached Letchworth. He would travel in the removal van.

Just as the removal van was ready to move off, Mr Pudney arrived with his taxicab to take us to Letchworth. Dad and Mr Pudney helped Granddad out and settled him comfortably first. Then Mum picked up Smut in his basket, and we all got into the taxi. It only remained for Dad to fetch Rover from the back garden where he had been chained to a tree in readiness for our departure. When we were all aboard, Mr Pudney took his seat at the wheel, glancing over his shoulder and said, "Right then, we're off."

"Say goodbye to Pengelly," Dad said.

"Goodbye, Pengelly," I said softly. My throat felt tight, and I swallowed hard and told myself, "I won't cry, I won't." Two large tears rolled down my cheeks and splashed on my coat, leaving two dark spots where they soaked into the material.

The bare windows seemed to stare at us like large, sad eyes, and I tore my gaze away and didn't look back.

We moved over the bumpy ground, and when we reached the road, many of our friends were there to wave us off, calling, "Good luck."

As we left the familiar fields and lanes, my spirits rose, and I began to anticipate the delights of our new home. Imagine having hot water for a bath without having to fill the copper and not having to dash across the yard to the lavatory in the rain. I began to warm to the idea of living in Letchworth.

After all, we were very lucky. We were going to live in a house where water came out of taps.

Epilogue

Fifty years later, I went back to visit Pengelly.

Whenever Mollie or Phyllis came to see me, inevitably our conversation turned to the good old days. Our nostalgia for Pengelly was so apparent that my husband became intrigued, and we decided to go and have a look at the old place.

We travelled by rail to Rayleigh Station, and as we alighted from the train, it was as though I had stepped back into the past. The station was exactly the same. It still had the slightly smoky, damp smell I remembered. The platforms were clean and free from litter, just the way they used to be.

Outside the station we took the road to our left and walked along past the house where Uncle Arnold lived.

I knew exactly where I was going and remembered every twist and turn of the road to Pengelly.

"When we get round the corner, we should be able to look across the fields and see the house in the distance," I told Michael. And sure enough, there it was. We continued on our way until we came to a cart track. I had expected to find a road with houses on each side, but no, it was just the same. We followed it across the fields, and then I was standing in front of Pengelly, still isolated with fields on every side. The only concession to modern life was the string of electric pylons, which had been erected.

The house itself had lost its splendour and had a somewhat neglected appearance. The balcony, veranda and large bay window were no longer there. No doubt the original limber had rotted, and the replacement windows were flat and ordinary. Yet it was unmistakably Pengelly.

Memories came crowding back into my mind. I could almost hear the happy laughter of those no longer with us, who had shared our days long ago. I had an absurd feeling that the house knew I was there.

Suddenly, I was a child again, and I led my husband around the hedgerows, recognising trees and footpaths.

"You'll lose us in a minute," he said.

"No, I won't. I know exactly where we are. The dragonfly pond is just along here," I replied. We found it, but the copse surrounding it had spread, enclosing it, until it was just a few yards wide. In fact, I would have passed it unnoticed, had I not been looking for it.

"Let's go and find my school," I said. I was amazed just how far it was from Pengelly. To think I had to walk there and back most days as a child. We walked along Watery Lane and then through a lane with tall trees on both sides and came to Hullbridge school. The school had been enlarged, but the original building remained, and I was grateful for that.

"What an extraordinary thing time is," I thought as I stood there. "One step back into the past at will, and the present becomes the future."

My only regret is that my brother, Eric, was born too late to share Pengelly with us. He entered the world two years after we left, and I have always felt he has been cheated out of those happy years.

"Never go back," friends told me. "It won't be the same."

But it was. It was wonderful.

Also available in ISIS Large Print:

We Waved to the Baker

Andrew Arbuckle

"I wished I had asked Mum to buy my most recent favourite food, a raisin-filled slice of cake that the baker called a 'fly cemetery'. This was rather a strange name because I never saw any dead flies when I was eating it."

We Waved to the Baker is an evocative and heart-warming collection of stories from Andrew Arbuckle's youth in Fife. Through the fresh gaze of childhood, he depicts the rugged hard work of life on the farm, while capturing the essence of growing up in a boisterous family and close rural community. We follow the young Andrew as he deals with the trials and tribulations of school, older brothers and plucking chickens, while throwing in as much mischief as possible.

ISBN 978-0-7531-9590-1 (hb)
ISBN 978-0-7531-9591-8 (pb)

Out With Romany Again

G. Bramwell Evens

"Tired of holding back the weight of the vardo, or possibly indignant of my lack of appreciation of all her caution, Comma tossed her head and broke into a trot. The brakes squealed, the pots and pans rattled and bounced on to the floor behind me, and Raq in the neighbouring field set up a howl of mingled astonishment and fear, as he saw the vardo rapidly vanishing from sight."

Romany returns to Fletcher's farm in his caravan with spaniel Raq in tow. Once again he and Tim, the farmer's son, will venture out into the countryside to discover new friends such as Sleek the Otter, Billy the Squirrel and Humphry the Mole. Through fictional tales told about these animals, and many more, learn the facts and real-life habits of some of Britain's best loved wildlife.

ISBN 978-0-7531-5253-9 (hb)
ISBN 978-0-7531-5254-6 (pb)

Poppies in the Corn

Fay Garrison

"My Father rented for us a rather run-down bungalow in the tiny Hamphire village of Redenham, a few miles from Andover. My mother, a city girl all her life, was horrified. Anything rural was anathema to her, from the dark country roads to the watchful cows in the fields."

When the Second World War broke out, Fay Garrison with her mother and sister moved from their native Birmingham. Her idyllic existence was then shattered by the news of her father's capture at Dunkirk.

Later in the war she returned to Birmingham, to a very different school system with new friends and teachers who shaped her future. A heroic aunt, captured by the Nazis who escaped to fight with the Resistance became a strong influence in her life. Eventually qualifying as a teacher she settled down in Solihull and married a journalist with whom she shared a love of music.

ISBN 978-0-7531-9576-5 (hb)
ISBN 978-0-7531-9577-2 (pb)

Strathalder

Roderick Grant

Strathalder is a wonderful evocation of life on a Scottish country estate from the 1920s to the 1970s.

"I was born and raised on a Scottish country estate where my father was a gamekeeper and my mother tended our home set in the heart of woodland close to the banks of a turbulent river. As a boy I was fortunate to have the freedom of thousands of acres in which to roam."

Based on hundreds of interviews with gardeners, gamekeepers, maids, governesses, lairds, chauffeurs, cooks and housekeepers, Roderick Grant creates a poignant and candid picture of a way of life which, although much changed, still survives in modern times. In addition to the harshness of work on the farms and the gradual transformation of the estate into a commercial business, we also learn much about the people themselves — their relationships with each other and those they worked for, and also their loyalties and disloyalties.

ISBN 978-0-7531-5241-6 (hb)
ISBN 978-0-7531-5242-3 (pb)

Not Far from Wigan Pier

Ted Dakin

Amusing tales reflecting a colourful childhood in Wigan

Ted Dakin was born in the 1930s in the Lancashire cotton town, Wigan. Far from living an idyll of times past, Ted grew up in a world of poverty, with a poor education at a tough Catholic school ruled by Owd Hector Wainwright's fist and cane. But the world he occupied was full of interesting people and amusing goings on.

In this delightful host of tales, he invokes the spirit of the time. He tells of skiving off Mass to avoid wearing a new suit so tight it felt like a second skin; of his Dad, reformed hypochondriac, self-taught herbalist and boxing trainer, and of the extraordinary Albert Crabtree, singer/coal miner, with his infamous renditions of "Danny Boy".

These nostalgic stories recreate the unity and values of a community and an age sadly long gone.

ISBN 978-0-7531-6479-2 (hb)
ISBN 978-0-7531-6480-8 (pb)